P9-DEQ-844

Market Math

Published by Time Inc. Books
1271 Avenue of the Americas • New York, NY 10020

Editor in Chief **Dana Cowin**
Executive Editor **Kate Heddings**
Editor **Susan Choung**
Recipe Contributors **Justin Chapple, Kay Chun, Ben Mims, Grace Parisi**
Wine Editor **Megan Krigbaum**
Copy Editor **Lisa Leventer**
Editorial Assistant **Kate Malczewski**

Creative Director **Fredrika Stjärne**
Designer **Courtney Eckersley**
Photo Editor **Sara Parks**
Production Director **Joseph Colucci**
Production Manager **Stephanie Thompson**

Principal Photography
(including front cover)
Photographer **Eva Kolenko**
Food Stylist **Lillian Kang**
Prop Stylist **Natasha Kolenko**

For additional photo contributors, see page 247.

ISBN 10: 0-8487-4693-7
ISBN 13: 978-0-8487-4693-3

Manufactured in the United States of America

By the Editors of
FOOD&**WINE**

Market Math

50 Ingredients
×4 Recipes
_____
200 Simple,
Creative Dishes

FOOD&**WINE**
BOOKS
Time Inc. Affluent Media Group, New York

Contents

Apples

13 Apple Sandwiches
13 Savory Apple Compote
14 Apples on Horseback
14 Caramel-Apple Ice Cream
15 Hard Cider Sangria

Apricots

16 Charred Green Beans
   with Apricots
17 Apricot and Ricotta Tartines
18 Honey-Thyme Chicken
   and Apricot Kebabs
19 Lemony Apricot Clafoutis

Asparagus

20 Asparagus Tabbouleh
20 Asparagus Pickles
22 Asparagus Vinaigrette
22 Pasta with Asparagus Pesto
23 Roasted Asparagus with
   Lemony Breadcrumbs

Avocado

24 Avocado Tartare
25 Avocado-Hummus Dip
27 Roasted Carrot and
   Avocado Salad
27 Alice Waters's Pink Grapefruit
   and Avocado Salad

Bananas

30 Banana-Strawberry Tartines
31 Tropical Banana Roast
32 Banana-Nut Truffles
33 Banana Snacking Cake

Beef

34 Steak Tacos with Pineapple
35 Spring Beef Stew
36 Grilled Rib Eye Steaks with
   Apple-Radish Vinaigrette
36 Sweet-and-Spicy Grilled Beef
   Short Ribs

Beets

38 Pickled Beets and Eggs
39 Salt-Baked Caraway Beets
39 Raw Beet and Kalamata
   Olive Relish
40 Beet and Lentil Salad with
   Beet Greens
40 Beet and Potato Latkes

Blueberries

42 Blueberry Dutch Baby
43 Blueberry Cheesecake Mousse
44 Blueberry Vinaigrette
45 Maraschino Blueberries

Broccoli

46 Flash-Roasted Broccoli
   with Spicy Crumbs
46 Creamy Roasted
   Broccoli Soup
48 Broccoli Cheese Dunk
48 Broccoli-Anchovy Fettuccine
49 Warm Kale and Broccoli Stem
   Salad with Leek Vinaigrette

Brussels Sprouts

50 Thai Brussels Sprout Salad
51 Brussels Sprout Frittata
53 Whole Roast Chicken with
   40 Brussels Sprouts
53 Spaghetti with Brussels
   Sprout and Sausage
   Breadcrumbs

Butternut Squash

54 Chipotle-Butternut Squash
   Soup with Chive Cream
55 Butternut Squash, Apple and
   Chicken Pan Roast
56 Squash Rösti Cakes with Sour
   Cream and Salmon Caviar
56 Mashed Butternut Squash
   with Roasted Garlic
57 Apricot-Glazed Butternut
   Squash Tart

Cabbage

61 Cabbage Slaw
61 Fresh Cabbage Kimchi
62 Chicken-Cabbage Salad
62 Potted Ham with Cabbage
   and Pickles
63 Tom Colicchio's Apple
   Cider-Braised Cabbage

Canned Tuna

64 Tuna Banh Mi
65 Tuscan White Bean and
   Escarole Soup with Tuna
66 Tuna Escabeche Tostadas
66 Lemony Tuna and
   Artichoke Dip

Recipes in **green** are star chef bonuses.

Carrots

69 Curry-Roasted Carrots with Carrot Top Gremolata

69 Nutty Carrot Pilaf

70 Crunchy Carrot and Beet Salad with Herbs

70 Carrot, Coconut and Zucchini Bread

71 Carrot-Pear Shrub

Cauliflower

73 Cauliflower Puree with Horseradish and Caraway

73 Silky Cauliflower Soup with Charmoula and Almonds

74 Stir-Fried Cauliflower "Rice"

74 Faux Tso's Cauliflower

Cherries

76 Israeli Couscous with Cherries and Olives

77 Cherry Hand Pies

78 Cherry-Lime Pudding Cups

78 Pork and Sausage Meat Loaf with Cherries

Chicken

81 Chicken Caesar Skewers

81 Sesame-Ginger Chicken Meatballs

82 Chicken Roasted on Bread with Caperberries

82 Chicken-Chile Soup

83 Michael Symon's Lemon-Shallot-Marinated Chicken

83 Bobby Flay's Honey Mustard Chicken

Chickpeas

84 Chickpea Salad Sandwiches

85 Chickpea and Swiss Chard Chili

86 Kale Caesar with Fried Chickpeas

87 Spanish-Style Chickpea Quesadillas

Corn

88 Skillet Corn with Bulgur

88 Corn-Shrimp Dumplings

91 Thai Glazed Corn

91 Parmesan Corn Butter

Cucumbers

92 Cucumber Gazpacho with Shrimp

93 Cucumber and Sugar Snap Salad with Nutty Granola

93 Cucumber and Salami Fried Rice with Arugula

94 Grilled Marinated Cucumbers and Eggplant with Basil

94 Bobby Flay's Dill Pickles

Eggplant

99 Pork and Eggplant Stir-Fry

99 Eggplant Noodle Salad

100 Grilled Eggplant Tortas

100 Eggplant Potato Salad

101 Jonathan Waxman's Baked Rigatoni with Eggplant, Tomatoes and Ricotta

Eggs

102 Mexican Eggs Baked in Tomato Sauce

103 Egg Salad with Herbs and Pickles

104 Cumin Oil–Fried Egg and Avocado Toasts

105 Sausage and Apple Frittata with Dill

Fish Fillets & Steaks

108 Smoky Fishwiches

109 Sea Bass Dill Meunière

110 Grilled Halibut Dip

110 Giada De Laurentiis's Swordfish Spiedini

111 Fish Soup with Cabbage and Potatoes

Grapes

114 Grape and Walnut Crostini with Roquefort

115 Roasted Grape Cake

116 Fresh Grape Soda

117 Grape Salsa Verde

Green Beans

118 Bloody Mary–Pickled Green Beans

119 Green Bean and Scallion Pancake

120 Sichuan-Style Green Beans with Pork

121 Tempura Green Beans with Old Bay and Lemon

Recipes in **green** are star chef bonuses.

Ground Beef

123 Adobo Meat Loaves

123 Yorkshire Pudding Bake with Beef and Cheddar

124 Coconut Curried Beef Noodles

125 Beet and Beef Burgers

Ham

129 Muffuletta Calzone

129 Spring Ham Steaks with Sweet Pea–Leek Pan Sauce

130 Open-Face Monte Cristos

130 Country Ham Flapjacks with Maple Syrup

131 Jose Garces's Ham, Escarole and White Bean Stew

Hot Peppers

132 Crispy Baked Jalapeño Poppers

133 Chile-Chicken Saltimbocca

134 Scallops with Thai Chile Sauce

135 Serrano Chile and Potato Hash

135 Rick Bayless's Chile-Cilantro Pesto

Kale

139 Nutty Baby Kale Chips

139 Kale Rice Bowl

140 Cacio e Pepe–Style Braised Kale

140 Garlicky Kale-and-Provolone Grinders

141 Marcus Samuelsson's Gingery Creamed Kale and Cabbage

Lamb

144 Coconut Lamb Curry with Sweet Potatoes

145 Simplest Lamb Bolognese with Pappardelle

146 Grilled Lamb Loin Chops with Pomegranate Relish

147 Spiced Lamb Sliders with Harissa Mayonnaise and Cucumber

Lentils

148 Warm Lentil and Carrot Salad with Feta Dressing

148 Yellow Lentil Dal with Tofu

150 Fried Spiced Red Lentils

150 Lentil and Chicken Cassoulet

Mushrooms

155 Mushroom Carpaccio with Chive Oil

155 Garlicky Mushroom Pasta with Parsley

156 Warm Mushroom–Barley Salad

157 Mushroom Poutine

Oranges

160 Honey-Orange Chicken

160 Roasted Orange Marmalade

162 Orange Caramel Sauce

163 Orange-Almond Parfaits

Pasta

166 Fettuccine with Shrimp

167 Cacio e Pepe Pasta Pie

168 Penne with Chicken and Pickled Peppers

169 Orecchiette with Sausage, Chickpeas and Mint

Peppers

171 Herb-Marinated Peppers and Tuna

171 Mixed Bell Pepper Pasta

172 Spicy Pickled Peppers

172 Bulgogi-Style Pepper Steak Sandwiches

173 Barbara Lynch's Chicken and Pepper Cacciatore

Pork

174 Spicy Fideos with Pork

175 Fennel-Rubbed Pork Tenderloin with Fingerling Potatoes and Lemon

177 Blackberry-Glazed Pork Chops with Broccolini

177 Vietnamese Pork Burgers

Potatoes

179 Warm Potato and Green Bean Salad

179 Crispy Buffalo-Style Potatoes

180 Accordion Potatoes

180 Potato-Apple-Dill Pancakes

181 Boiled Potatoes with Sage Butter

181 Mario Batali's Tortilla Española

Quinoa

185 Quinoa Pilaf with Dates, Olives and Arugula

185 Skirt Steak Quinoa Bowls with Ginger-Sesame Dressing

186 Quinoa-Dill Omelet with Feta

187 Quinoa-Pork Meatballs

Recipes in **green** are star chef bonuses.

Rice

191 Coconut Rice Salad

191 Baked Shrimp Risotto

192 Indian Fried Rice with Chickpeas and Spinach

192 Spiced Rice Breakfast Porridge

193 José Andrés's Rice Pudding Brûlée

Salmon

197 Salmon and Citrus Salad with Poppy Seed Dressing

197 Salmon, Broccolini and Fresh Red Chile Papillotes

198 Salmon and Cherry Tomato Skewers with Rosemary Vinaigrette

198 Salmon Sandwiches with Bacon and Apple-Horseradish Mayo

Sausage

200 Sausage and Cheddar Muffins

201 Sausage Choucroute

202 Sausage and Fennel Parm Heroes

203 Warm Escarole Salad with Sausage Vinaigrette

Shrimp

204 Shrimp and Chorizo Tortas

204 Shrimp Salad with Green Curry Dressing

206 Shrimp Cakes with Spicy Mayo

206 Angry Shrimp Spaghettini

207 Stephanie Izard's Grilled Shrimp with Shrimp Butter

Snap Peas

208 Double-Pea Sauté with Ground Pork

209 Warm Snap Peas with Ham and Tarragon Butter

211 Snap Pea and Radish Salad with Tahini Dressing

211 Snap Pea Falafel Salad

Spinach

213 Quinoa with Spinach and Roasted Almonds

213 Spinach and Caramelized Onion Dip

214 Spinach Salad with Walnut Vinaigrette

214 Asian Pork Noodles with Spinach

215 Tanya Holland's Spinach Spoon Bread

Strawberries

216 Caramelized Panzanella with Strawberries

217 Strawberry-Prosecco Gelées

218 Strawberry Shortcake

219 Fresh Strawberry Sauce

219 Mario Batali's Balsamic Strawberries with Strawberry Sorbet

Sweet Potatoes

220 Sweet Potato Hash Browns

220 Sweet Potato-Tomato Pasta Sauce

222 Sweet Potatoes with Almond Pesto

222 Sweet Potato and Mushroom Salad

223 Baked Sweet Potato Chips

Tofu

227 Creamy Sesame-Garlic Tofu Dressing

227 Seared Tofu Tabbouleh

228 Crispy Tofu Steaks with Ginger Vinaigrette

229 Tofu Masala

Tomatoes

230 Summery Fresh Tomato Soup

230 Roasted Tomatoes with Anchovies and Capers

232 Pappardelle with Tomatoes, Almonds and Parmesan

233 Tomato Salad with Horseradish Ranch Dressing

234 Garlic-Toasted Tomato Tartines

234 Jacques Pépin's Garlicky Cherry Tomato and Bread Gratin

Turkey

237 Turkey Tonnato

237 Turkey Curry Soup

238 Turkey-Stuffing Salad

238 Turkey Reuben Hash

239 Art Smith's Turkey and Pinto Bean Chili

Zucchini

242 Zucchini Gratin

242 Zucchini Confetti Pasta with Dill and Walnuts

245 Grilled Zucchini and Lamb with Serrano Chile

245 Crispy Zucchini Pancakes

Recipes in **green** are star chef bonuses.

For anyone who has ever gotten carried away at the market and returned home with way too many carrots...

Market Math, based on FOOD & WINE magazine's super-popular column of the same name, can help. This book shows our tremendous enthusiasm for everyday ingredients–carrots, definitely, as well as chicken, quinoa and kale (the three most searched ingredients online!). The recipes come from the amazing cooks in our Test Kitchen. They selected 50 ingredients from the greenmarket or supermarket–items like canned tuna, eggs, spinach and apples–and created four simple, delicious, completely different dishes for each.

For additional clever yet doable ideas, we tapped our chef friends for recipes. We've translated their professional tricks for the home kitchen. A few examples: cherry tomato and bread gratin from Jacques Pépin, swordfish spiedini from Giada De Laurentiis and pink grapefruit and avocado salad from Alice Waters.

We love how *Market Math* combines familiar flavors and inspiring ideas, and hope you do too. Let us know how your recipes turned out via Twitter and Instagram @foodandwine, using the hashtag #marketmath.

Editor in Chief
FOOD & WINE

Executive Editor
FOOD & WINE Cookbooks

Apples

13   Apple Sandwiches

13   Savory Apple Compote

14   Apples on Horseback

14   Caramel-Apple Ice Cream

15   Hard Cider Sangria

Apricots

16   Charred Green Beans with Apricots

17   Apricot and Ricotta Tartines

18   Honey-Thyme Chicken and Apricot Kebabs

19   Lemony Apricot Clafoutis

Asparagus

20   Asparagus Tabbouleh

20   Asparagus Pickles

22   Asparagus Vinaigrette

22   Pasta with Asparagus Pesto

23   Roasted Asparagus with Lemony Breadcrumbs

Avocado

24   Avocado Tartare

25   Avocado-Hummus Dip

27   Roasted Carrot and Avocado Salad

27   Pink Grapefruit and Avocado Salad

Apple Sandwiches

Savory Apple Compote

Apples on Horseback, p. 14

Caramel-Apple Ice Cream, p. 14

Apple Sandwiches

Total **5 min**; Serves **1**

1 apple, thinly sliced
   horizontally

2 Tbsp. almond butter

2 Tbsp. granola

Spread the apple slices with the almond butter and sprinkle half of them with the granola. Close the sandwiches and eat right away.

Variation Substitute another nut butter, such as peanut or cashew, for the almond butter.

Savory Apple Compote

Total **30 min**; Makes **1½ cups**

1 Tbsp. unsalted butter

⅓ cup minced Vidalia or
   other sweet onion

4 Empire apples, peeled and
   finely chopped

1½ tsp. minced crystallized ginger

   Pinch of dried sage

2 Tbsp. apple cider vinegar

2 Tbsp. sugar

   Salt

Melt the butter in a medium saucepan. Add the onion and cook over moderate heat, stirring, until softened, about 4 minutes. Add the apples, ginger, sage, vinegar, sugar and ¼ cup of water and bring to a boil. Cover and cook over low heat, stirring and mashing occasionally, until the apples are very tender, about 10 minutes. Season the compote with salt.

Serve With Pork chops, ham steaks or turkey burgers with sweet pickles and grainy mustard.

Apples on Horseback

Total **30 min**; Makes **16 pieces**

16 thin slices of pancetta

1 Pink Lady apple, peeled and
cut into 16 wedges

3 oz. Manchego cheese, sliced
¼ inch thick and cut into
sixteen 2-by-½-inch sticks

Sixteen 2-inch rosemary sprigs
or toothpicks

1. Heat a grill pan. Arrange the pancetta slices on a work surface and place an apple wedge and a cheese stick in the center of each slice. Wrap the pancetta around the filling and secure with a rosemary sprig or toothpick.

2. Grill the skewers until the pancetta is golden and crispy and the cheese is melted, 5 to 6 minutes. Serve hot.

Wine Lively, fruit-forward sparkling wine.

Caramel-Apple Ice Cream

Total **20 min plus 4 hr freezing**
Serves **4 or 5**

2 Tbsp. unsalted butter

2 Granny Smith apples–peeled,
quartered and very thinly sliced

1 Tbsp. sugar

⅛ tsp. cinnamon

¼ cup dulce de leche

2 pints vanilla ice cream, softened

Chocolate shavings and
crumbled gingersnaps,
for garnish

1. Melt the butter in a medium skillet. Add the apples and cook over moderate heat, stirring, until softened and lightly browned, about 5 minutes. Add the sugar, cinnamon and ¼ cup of water and cook for 2 minutes longer. Stir in the dulce de leche until melted. Scrape the apple mixture into a medium bowl and refrigerate until chilled.

2. Fold the softened ice cream into the apple mixture and freeze until firm, about 4 hours. Scoop into bowls and garnish with chocolate shavings and crumbled gingersnaps.

Hard Cider Sangria

Total **15 min**; Serves **4**

- 1 **cup quartered and thinly sliced unpeeled apples**
- 1 **navel orange, quartered and thinly sliced crosswise**
- 1 **cup chilled apple juice**
- ¼ **cup apple brandy**
- 2 **Tbsp. fresh lemon juice**
- 1 **chilled 22-oz. bottle hard apple cider**
- **Ice**

In a pitcher, combine the apple and orange slices with the apple juice, brandy and lemon juice. Just before serving, stir in the hard cider. Serve in tall glasses over ice.

Charred Green Beans with Apricots

Total **20 min**; Serves **4**

1½ **Tbsp. canola oil**

½ **lb. haricots verts**

3 **apricots–halved, pitted and cut into ½-inch wedges**

2 **Tbsp. fresh lime juice**

1 **Tbsp. Asian fish sauce**

1 **Thai chile, thinly sliced**

1 **lightly packed cup mint leaves**

Salt

In a large skillet, heat the oil until shimmering. Add the beans and cook over high heat until charred on the bottom, about 4 minutes. Remove from the heat and stir in the apricots, lime juice, fish sauce, chile and mint. Season with salt, transfer to a platter and serve.

Apricot and Ricotta Tartines

Total **30 min**; Serves 4

- 4 slices of sourdough bread
- 1 Tbsp. extra-virgin olive oil, plus more for brushing
- 4 apricots, halved and pitted
- Salt and pepper
- 1 cup yellow and red cherry tomatoes, halved
- 3 Tbsp. Champagne vinegar
- 1½ Tbsp. chopped tarragon
- 1 cup fresh ricotta cheese

1. Light a grill or heat a grill pan. Brush the bread with olive oil and grill over high heat until toasted and charred in spots, about 1 minute per side. Transfer to a work surface.

2. Brush the apricot halves with olive oil and season with salt and pepper. Grill cut side down over high heat until charred on the bottom, about 3 minutes. Transfer to a work surface and let cool slightly, then cut into ½-inch wedges.

3. In a medium bowl, toss the apricots with the tomatoes, vinegar, tarragon and the 1 tablespoon of olive oil. Season the salad with salt and pepper. Spread the ricotta on the grilled bread and spoon the apricot salad on top. Serve right away.

Wine Juicy, vibrant Spanish rosé.

Honey-Thyme Chicken and Apricot Kebabs

Total **45 min**; Serves **4**

¼ cup honey

1 Tbsp. chopped thyme leaves

Salt and pepper

1 lb. skinless, boneless chicken thighs, cut into 1-inch pieces

4 apricots—halved, pitted and cut into 1-inch pieces

12 long wooden skewers, soaked in water for 30 minutes

Extra-virgin olive oil, for brushing

1. In a small bowl, whisk the honey with 1 tablespoon of water and the thyme. Season with salt and pepper.

2. Light a grill or heat a grill pan. Thread the chicken and apricots onto the skewers. Brush the kebabs with olive oil and season with salt and pepper. Grill over moderate heat, turning occasionally, until the chicken is just cooked through, about 10 minutes. Transfer the kebabs to a platter, brush with the honey-thyme mixture and serve.

Wine Fruit-forward, lightly off-dry German Riesling.

Lemony Apricot Clafoutis

Active **15 min**; Total **1 hr**; Serves **4**

 3 **large eggs**

 ½ **cup granulated sugar**

 ½ **cup half-and-half**

 3 **Tbsp. all-purpose flour**

1½ **Tbsp. finely grated lemon zest**
    (from 1 lemon)

 ¾ **tsp. kosher salt**

 4 **apricots–halved, pitted and**
    cut into wedges

    Confectioners' sugar, for dusting

Preheat the oven to 350°. In a large bowl, beat the eggs with the granulated sugar, half-and-half, flour, lemon zest and salt until very smooth. Pour the batter into a 1-quart gratin dish or a 9-inch ceramic pie plate and arrange the apricots on top. Bake for about 30 minutes, until the custard is just set. Let stand for 10 minutes, then dust with confectioners' sugar and serve.

Asparagus Tabbouleh

Total **20 min**; Serves **4**

⅓ **cup medium-grind bulgur**

1 **lb. asparagus, trimmed**

1 **small tomato, chopped**

¼ **cup chopped flat-leaf parsley**

2 **scallions, thinly sliced**

2 **Tbsp. finely chopped mint**

2 **Tbsp. extra-virgin olive oil**

1 **Tbsp. fresh lemon juice**

Salt and pepper

1. In a medium saucepan of boiling water, cook the bulgur until tender, about 10 minutes. Drain well, then spread out on a rimmed baking sheet to cool.

2. Meanwhile, fill a medium bowl with ice water. In a large pot of salted boiling water, blanch the asparagus for 2 minutes, then transfer to the ice bath to cool. Drain, coarsely chop and transfer to a food processor. Pulse the asparagus until it is finely chopped.

3. In a large bowl, combine the asparagus with the bulgur, tomato, parsley, scallions, mint, olive oil and lemon juice and toss. Season with salt and pepper and serve.

Asparagus Pickles

Total **20 min plus overnight pickling**
Makes **two 24-ounce jars**

2 **lbs. asparagus, trimmed**

6 **dill sprigs**

1 **quart distilled white vinegar**

¼ **cup kosher salt**

2 **Tbsp. sugar**

12 **dried red chiles,
    such as chiles de árbol**

12 **garlic cloves, crushed**

2 **Tbsp. whole black peppercorns**

2 **Tbsp. mustard seeds**

Divide the asparagus and dill between two 24-ounce containers or jars. In a large saucepan, combine the vinegar with 1 quart of water and all of the remaining ingredients. Bring to a boil and simmer for 10 minutes, stirring to dissolve the salt and sugar. Let stand at room temperature until the brine is lukewarm. Pour over the asparagus (reserve any remaining brine for another use), cover and refrigerate overnight for fresh pickles or 3 days for stronger pickles.

Asparagus Tabbouleh

Asparagus Pickles

Asparagus Vinaigrette, p. 22

Pasta with Asparagus Pesto,
p. 22

Asparagus Vinaigrette

Total **15 min**; Makes **1 cup**

1 lb. asparagus, trimmed

1 Tbsp. Dijon mustard

1 Tbsp. fresh lemon juice

1 Tbsp. chopped chives

¾ cup grapeseed or canola oil

Salt and pepper

Fill a medium bowl with ice water. In a pot of salted boiling water, blanch the asparagus for 2 minutes, then transfer to the ice bath to cool. Drain, chop and transfer the asparagus to a food processor. Add the mustard, lemon juice and chives and pulse until finely chopped. With the machine on, add the oil in a steady stream until well blended. Strain through a fine sieve; discard the solids. Season the vinaigrette with salt and pepper.

Serve With Salad greens, grilled steak or roast chicken.

Pasta with Asparagus Pesto

Total **30 min**; Serves **4**

¾ pound spaghetti

1 lb. asparagus, trimmed and coarsely chopped

½ cup extra-virgin olive oil, plus more for drizzling

¼ cup freshly grated Parmigiano-Reggiano cheese

½ cup basil leaves, torn if large

1 Tbsp. fresh lemon juice

Salt and pepper

1. In a large pot of salted boiling water, cook the pasta until al dente. Drain, reserving ¼ cup of the pasta cooking water.

2. Meanwhile, in a food processor, pulse the asparagus until finely chopped. Transfer to a large bowl. Stir in the ½ cup of olive oil along with the cheese, basil and lemon juice; season the pesto with salt and pepper. Add the hot pasta and reserved cooking water and toss until the pasta is well coated with pesto. Season with salt and pepper, drizzle with olive oil and serve.

Wine Tangy, medium-bodied Austrian Grüner Veltliner.

Roasted Asparagus with Lemony Breadcrumbs

Active **15 min**; Total **30 min**
Serves **6 to 8**

- 2 lbs. white and/or green asparagus
- ⅓ cup plus 2 Tbsp. extra-virgin olive oil
-    Salt and pepper
- 7 anchovy fillets in oil, drained and chopped
- 2 garlic cloves, minced
- 1 cup panko
- 1 Tbsp. chopped flat-leaf parsley
- 2 tsp. finely grated lemon zest
-    Juice of 1 lemon, for drizzling

1. Preheat the oven to 425°. On a baking sheet, toss the asparagus with 2 tablespoons of the olive oil and season with salt and pepper. Roast for 20 to 25 minutes, turning once, until golden and tender.

2. Meanwhile, in a small skillet, simmer the remaining ⅓ cup of olive oil with the anchovies over moderate heat, stirring, until the anchovies dissolve. Add the garlic and cook for 1 minute. Stir in the panko and cook, stirring frequently, until golden and crispy, about 5 minutes. Stir in the parsley and lemon zest.

3. Transfer the roasted asparagus to a platter. Drizzle with lemon juice, top with the lemony panko and serve.

Avocado Tartare

Total **20 min**; Serves 4

- **2** Tbsp. extra-virgin olive oil
- **2** Tbsp. minced red onion
- **1** Tbsp. fresh lemon juice
- **1** Tbsp. drained capers
- **1** Tbsp. chopped parsley
- **1** Tbsp. Dijon mustard, plus more for garnish (optional)
- **½** small jalapeño, minced
- **3** drops of Worcestershire sauce

  Salt and pepper
- **2** medium Hass avocados, finely diced

In a medium bowl, stir the olive oil with the onion, lemon juice, capers, parsley and the 1 tablespoon of mustard. Stir in the jalapeño and Worcestershire sauce and season with salt and pepper. Gently fold in the avocados. Mound the tartare on plates and dollop some mustard in the center of each serving.

Serve With Toasted baguette slices.

Wine Citrusy, medium-bodied Spanish white, such as Verdejo.

Avocado-Hummus Dip

Total **15 min**; Makes **2½ cups**

2 **medium Hass avocados, chopped**

   One 15-oz. can chickpeas, rinsed

¼ **cup fresh lemon juice**

1½ **Tbsp. tahini**

½ **cup extra-virgin olive oil, plus more for drizzling**

   Salt and pepper

   Assorted crudités, bread and tortilla chips, for serving

In a food processor, puree the avocados with the chickpeas, lemon juice and tahini. Add the ½ cup of oil and puree until smooth; season with salt and pepper. Transfer the dip to a bowl, drizzle with olive oil and serve with crudités, bread or tortilla chips.

Roasted Carrot and Avocado Salad

Roasted Carrot and Avocado Salad

Total **45 min**; Serves **4 to 6**

¼ **cup plus 2 Tbsp.
extra-virgin olive oil**

3 **Tbsp. fresh grapefruit juice
plus 2 tsp. finely grated
grapefruit zest**

1½ **tsp. ground coriander**

1½ **lbs. medium carrots,
cut into ¼-inch-thick rounds**

Salt and pepper

¼ **cup roasted almonds, chopped**

⅓ **cup chopped parsley**

2 **medium Hass avocados,
cut into wedges**

1. Preheat the oven to 450°. In a small bowl, whisk the olive oil with the grapefruit juice and coriander.

2. On a rimmed baking sheet, toss the carrots with 3 tablespoons of the dressing. Spread the carrots in a single layer and roast for about 20 minutes, turning once, until golden and tender. Season with salt and pepper.

3. In a small bowl, mix the almonds with the grapefruit zest and parsley. Arrange the roasted carrots and the avocados on a platter. Drizzle with the remaining dressing, top with the grapefruit gremolata and serve.

BONUS RECIPE BY CHEF ALICE WATERS

Pink Grapefruit and Avocado Salad

Total **30 min**; Serves **4**

2 **medium pink grapefruits**

1 **tsp. finely grated
grapefruit zest**

1 **medium shallot, minced**

1 **tsp. white wine vinegar**

2 **medium Hass avocados,
sliced ¼ inch thick**

Salt

2 **Tbsp. extra-virgin olive oil**

Pepper

Chervil leaves, for garnish

1. Using a sharp knife, cut the skin and all of the bitter white pith off the grapefruits. Working over a bowl, cut in between the membranes to release the sections. Squeeze the juice from the membranes into the bowl.

2. Transfer 2 tablespoons of the juice to another bowl. Add the zest, shallot and vinegar; let the dressing stand for 10 minutes.

3. Season the avocados with salt and arrange on plates with the grapefruit sections. Stir the oil into the dressing and season with salt and pepper. Drizzle onto the grapefruit and avocado, garnish with chervil and serve.

Bananas

30	Banana-Strawberry Tartines
31	Tropical Banana Roast
32	Banana-Nut Truffles
33	Banana Snacking Cake

Beef

34	Steak Tacos with Pineapple
35	Spring Beef Stew
36	Grilled Rib Eye Steaks with Apple-Radish Vinaigrette
36	Sweet-and-Spicy Grilled Beef Short Ribs

Beets

38	Pickled Beets and Eggs
39	Salt-Baked Caraway Beets
39	Raw Beet and Kalamata Olive Relish
40	Beet and Lentil Salad with Beet Greens
40	Beet and Potato Latkes

Blueberries

42	Blueberry Dutch Baby
43	Blueberry Cheesecake Mousse
44	Blueberry Vinaigrette
45	Maraschino Blueberries

Broccoli

46	Flash-Roasted Broccoli with Spicy Crumbs
46	Creamy Roasted Broccoli Soup
48	Broccoli Cheese Dunk
48	Broccoli-Anchovy Fettuccine
49	Warm Kale and Broccoli Stem Salad with Leek Vinaigrette

Brussels Sprouts

50	Thai Brussels Sprout Salad
51	Brussels Sprout Frittata
53	Whole Roast Chicken with 40 Brussels Sprouts
53	Spaghetti with Brussels Sprout and Sausage Breadcrumbs

Butternut Squash

54	Chipotle-Butternut Squash Soup with Chive Cream
55	Butternut Squash, Apple and Chicken Pan Roast
56	Squash Rösti Cakes with Sour Cream and Salmon Caviar
56	Mashed Butternut Squash with Roasted Garlic
57	Apricot-Glazed Butternut Squash Tart

Banana-Strawberry Tartines

Total **10 min**; Serves **2**

- ¹/₂ **cup Greek yogurt**
- 1 **banana–half mashed, half sliced ¹/₄ inch thick**
- 2 **large slices of toast**
- 4 **strawberries, thinly sliced**
- 2 **Tbsp. honey**
- ¹/₂ **tsp. poppy seeds**

In a medium bowl, stir the yogurt with the mashed banana. Spoon the banana yogurt onto the toasts and top them with the sliced strawberries and sliced banana. Drizzle the toasts with the honey, sprinkle with the poppy seeds and serve.

Tropical Banana Roast

Active **15 min**; Total **1 hr**
Serves **2**

- 2 ripe bananas, peeled
- 2 tsp. honey
- ¼ tsp. kosher salt
- ¼ cup unsweetened coconut milk
- 1 Tbsp. fresh lime juice
- 2 Tbsp. toasted coconut flakes
- ½ tsp. finely grated lime zest
    Vanilla ice cream, for serving

1. Preheat the oven to 400°. Halve each banana crosswise and then halve each piece lengthwise to create 8 banana quarters. Place the bananas in a 9-inch pie pan, drizzle with the honey and sprinkle with the salt. Bake for 25 minutes, until caramelized.

2. Pour the coconut milk and lime juice over the bananas and bake for 15 minutes, until the bananas are soft and the coconut milk is reduced by about one-third. In a small bowl, toss the coconut flakes with the lime zest and sprinkle over the bananas. Serve warm, with vanilla ice cream.

Banana-Nut Truffles

Total **30 min plus 1 hr chilling**
Makes **3 dozen truffles**

3½ oz. bittersweet chocolate, melted and cooled

½ cup creamy peanut butter

1 banana

½ cup chopped smoked almonds

Unsweetened cocoa powder, for coating

1. In a food processor, combine the melted chocolate with the peanut butter and banana and puree until smooth. Scrape into a medium bowl and stir in the almonds.

2. Spread the cocoa powder in a pie plate. Roll the chocolate-peanut butter mixture into 1-inch balls, then roll them in the cocoa powder until evenly coated. Arrange the truffles on a baking sheet and chill until firm, at least 1 hour.

Make Ahead The truffles can be refrigerated for up to 3 days.

Banana Snacking Cake

Active **15 min**; Total **1 hr 10 min**
Serves **8 to 10**

    Butter, for greasing

1¼ **cups self-rising flour,
plus more for dusting**

 ⅔ **cup extra-virgin olive oil**

 ⅔ **cup pure maple syrup**

 3 **large eggs**

 1 **banana, sliced on the diagonal
½ inch thick**

    Confectioners' sugar, for dusting

1. Preheat the oven to 350°. Grease and flour an 8-inch round baking pan and line the bottom with parchment paper. In a large bowl, whisk the olive oil with the maple syrup and eggs until smooth. Stir in the 1¼ cups of flour and the banana.

2. Scrape the batter into the prepared pan and bake for 45 minutes, until golden brown and a toothpick inserted in the center comes out clean. Let cool for 10 minutes. Unmold the cake and dust with confectioners' sugar. Serve warm or at room temperature.

Make Ahead The cake can be kept in an airtight container at room temperature overnight.

Steak Tacos with Pineapple

Total **45 min**; Serves **4**

- **3 Tbsp. soy sauce**
- **1 Tbsp. finely grated garlic**
- **1 Tbsp. finely grated peeled fresh ginger**
- **1½ lbs. skirt steak, cut into 5-inch lengths**
- **Salt and pepper**
- **Warm corn tortillas, diced fresh pineapple, thinly sliced red onion and cilantro leaves, for serving**

1. In a small bowl, whisk the soy sauce with the garlic and ginger. Brush the mixture all over the steak and season lightly with salt and pepper. Let stand for 20 minutes.

2. Heat a large cast-iron skillet. Add the steak and cook over high heat, turning once, until charred on the outside and medium-rare within, about 6 minutes. Transfer to a carving board and let rest for 5 minutes. Carve the steak against the grain and serve in warm corn tortillas with diced pineapple, sliced red onion and cilantro leaves.

Beer Crisp, lightly toasty amber ale.

Spring Beef Stew

Active **30 min**; Total **2 hr**
Serves **4 to 6**

- 2 Tbsp. extra-virgin olive oil
- 2 lbs. beef chuck, cut into 1½-inch pieces
- Salt and pepper
- 1 qt. chicken stock or low-sodium broth
- 6 shallots, halved
- ½ lb. carrots, cut into 2-inch lengths
- 1½ cups frozen peas
- 5 oz. curly spinach
- 2 Tbsp. chopped dill
- Crusty bread, for serving

1. In a large saucepan, heat the olive oil until shimmering. Season the meat with salt and pepper and add it to the saucepan in a single layer. Cook over moderately high heat, turning occasionally, until browned all over, about 10 minutes. Add the stock and shallots and bring to a boil. Simmer over low heat until the meat is tender, about 1½ hours.

2. Add the carrots to the saucepan and simmer until tender, about 12 minutes. Add the peas, spinach and dill and cook until the spinach is wilted, about 2 minutes. Ladle the stew into bowls and serve with crusty bread.

Make Ahead The stew can be refrigerated overnight. Reheat gently before serving.

Grilled Rib Eye Steaks with Apple-Radish Vinaigrette

Total **30 min**; Serves **4**

⅓ cup extra-virgin olive oil, plus more for oiling the grate and brushing the steaks

Two 1-inch-thick boneless rib eye steaks (1½ lbs. total), at room temperature

Salt and pepper

3 Tbsp. Champagne vinegar

¼ cup minced radish

¼ cup minced crisp, sweet apple, such as Honeycrisp

1. Light a grill and oil the grate. Brush the steaks all over with olive oil and season generously with salt and pepper. Grill over moderately high heat, turning once, until medium-rare, 6 to 8 minutes. Transfer to a carving board and let rest for 5 minutes.

2. Meanwhile, in a medium bowl, mix the ⅓ cup of olive oil with the vinegar, radish and apple. Season the vinaigrette with salt and pepper. Carve the steaks against the grain and serve with the vinaigrette.

Wine Lively, medium-bodied red, such as Spanish Garnacha.

Sweet-and-Spicy Grilled Beef Short Ribs

Total **45 min**; Serves **4**

¼ cup packed light brown sugar

1½ Tbsp. kosher salt

1 Tbsp. paprika

1 Tbsp. chili powder

1 tsp. garlic salt

1 tsp. dried oregano

1 tsp. black pepper

3¾ lbs. flanken-style beef short ribs, sliced ⅓ inch thick

Canola oil, for oiling the grate

Lemon wedges, for serving

1. In a medium bowl, mix all of the ingredients except the short ribs, oil and lemon. Rub the mixture all over the short ribs and let stand for 20 minutes.

2. Light a grill and oil the grate. Grill the ribs over high heat, turning once, until nicely charred and nearly cooked through, about 6 minutes. Transfer to a platter and serve with lemon wedges.

Make Ahead The spice rub can be stored in an airtight container for up to 1 month.

Serve With Coleslaw.

Wine Dark-berried, full-bodied Argentinean Malbec.

Grilled Rib Eye Steaks with
Apple-Radish Vinaigrette

Pickled Beets and Eggs

Active **25 min**; Total **3 hr 30 min plus overnight pickling**; Serves 4

- 4 **small red beets (about ¾ lb.), scrubbed**
- 1 **cup raw, unfiltered apple cider vinegar**
- 3 **garlic cloves, crushed**
- 3 **Tbsp. sugar**
- 2 **tsp. whole black peppercorns**
- 1 **Tbsp. kosher salt**
- 1 **small red onion, cut into thin wedges**
- 4 **hard-boiled large eggs, peeled**
- 6 **dill sprigs**

1. Preheat the oven to 450°. Wrap the beets in foil and roast for about 1 hour, until tender. When cool enough to handle, slip off the skins and quarter the beets.

2. Meanwhile, in a medium saucepan, combine the vinegar and 1 cup of water with the garlic, sugar, peppercorns and salt. Bring to a boil and simmer over moderately high heat, stirring, until the sugar is dissolved, about 5 minutes. Let the pickling liquid cool to warm, about 15 minutes.

3. Layer the beets, onion, eggs and dill in a 1-quart heatproof glass jar and cover with the pickling liquid. Let stand at room temperature for 2 hours. Cover and refrigerate overnight before serving.

Make Ahead The pickled beets and eggs can be refrigerated for up to 1 week.

Salt-Baked Caraway Beets

Active **15 min**; Total **1 hr**
Serves **4**

4 cups kosher salt

2 Tbsp. caraway seeds

¼ cup chopped sage leaves,
   plus 5 sage sprigs

3 bunches of mixed baby beets
   (1¼ lbs. or about 15 baby
   beets), trimmed and scrubbed

   Whole-milk Greek yogurt or
   sour cream, for serving

1. Preheat the oven to 350°. In a large bowl, mix the salt with the caraway seeds and chopped sage. In a large baking dish, spread 1 cup of the salt mixture in an even layer. Lay the beets and sage sprigs on the salt and cover them completely with the remaining salt mixture. Bake for about 40 minutes, or until the beets are tender when pierced with a knife.

2. Crack the salt crust and remove the beets. Dust off the salt and slip off the skins. Wipe off any excess salt with paper towels and serve the baked beets with yogurt.

Raw Beet and Kalamata Olive Relish

Total **20 min**; Makes **about 2 cups**

2 medium beets (½ lb.), peeled
   and grated on the large holes
   of a box grater

½ cup pitted kalamata olives,
   chopped

¼ cup chopped parsley

¼ cup chopped basil

¼ cup extra-virgin olive oil

1 Tbsp. fresh lemon juice

In a medium bowl, combine all of the ingredients and mix well.

Serve With Roast chicken or grilled steak, or use as a sandwich topping.

Make Ahead The relish can be refrigerated for up to 3 days.

Beet and Lentil Salad with Beet Greens

Active **15 min**; Total **1 hr 15 min**
Serves **4**

2 medium golden beets with nice leafy greens (about 1 lb.), stems discarded, greens reserved

1 cup French green (Le Puy) lentils, rinsed and drained

6 Tbsp. extra-virgin olive oil

2 Tbsp. Dijon mustard

2 Tbsp. fresh lemon juice

2 scallions, thinly sliced

Salt and pepper

1. Preheat the oven to 450°. Wrap the beets in foil and roast for about 1 hour, until tender. When cool enough to handle, slip off the skins and cut the beets into wedges. Tear the beet greens into bite-size pieces; you should have about 2 cups.

2. Meanwhile, in a medium saucepan of boiling water, cook the lentils until tender, about 20 minutes. Drain and cool under running water; drain well.

3. In a large bowl, whisk the olive oil with the mustard, lemon juice and scallions. Add the lentils, beets and beet greens and season with salt and pepper; toss and serve.

Wine Crisp, lemony Sauvignon Blanc.

Beet and Potato Latkes

Total **45 min**; Makes **6 latkes**

1 large baking potato (³/₄ lb.)– peeled, julienned on a mandoline and patted dry

2 medium beets (¹/₂ lb.)–peeled, julienned on a mandoline and patted dry

¹/₄ cup all-purpose flour

1 Tbsp. thyme leaves

¹/₂ tsp. freshly ground pepper

Kosher salt

2 large eggs, lightly beaten

¹/₄ cup canola oil

Sour cream, for serving

1. In a large bowl, toss the julienned potato and beets with the flour, thyme, pepper and 1 teaspoon of kosher salt. Add the eggs and mix well.

2. In a large nonstick skillet, heat 1 tablespoon of the canola oil until shimmering. Spoon three ¹/₂-cup mounds of the latke mixture into the hot oil and press lightly to flatten. Fry over moderate heat, turning once and adding 1 tablespoon of oil, until the latkes are golden and crisp on both sides, about 15 minutes. Repeat with the remaining latke mixture and 2 tablespoons of oil. Drain on paper towels and sprinkle with salt. Serve with sour cream.

Wine Fresh, berry-scented sparkling rosé.

Beet and Lentil Salad
with Beet Greens

Blueberry Dutch Baby

Total **30 min**; Serves **4**

³⁄₄ **cup all-purpose flour**

¹⁄₂ **cup whole milk**

¹⁄₄ **cup pomegranate juice**

3 **large eggs**

6 **Tbsp. salted butter**

1 **cup blueberries**

Confectioners' sugar, for dusting

Preheat the oven to 425°. In a large bowl, whisk the flour with the milk, pomegranate juice and eggs until blended. In a 12-inch ovenproof skillet, melt the butter over high heat until foamy. Pour in the batter and sprinkle on the blueberries. Transfer the skillet to the oven and bake for 20 minutes, until the pancake is golden brown. Dust with confectioners' sugar and serve immediately.

Blueberry Cheesecake Mousse

Active **30 min**; Total **1 hr**; Serves **6**

- 1 cup blueberries,
  plus more for garnish
- ½ cup sugar
- 1 tsp. kosher salt
- 1 cup sour cream
- 8 oz. cream cheese, softened
- 1 cup chilled heavy cream
  Chopped pistachios,
  for garnish

1. In a small saucepan, mash the 1 cup of blueberries with the sugar and salt and bring to a simmer over moderate heat. Cook, stirring, until jammy, about 10 minutes. Remove from the heat and scrape the jam into a food processor. Let cool completely.

2. Add the sour cream and cream cheese to the food processor and puree with the jam until smooth. In a large bowl, beat the heavy cream to soft peaks. Fold in the berry cream until blended. Spoon the mousse into glasses, sprinkle with pistachios and blueberries and serve.

Make Ahead The mousse can be prepared through Step 1 and refrigerated overnight.

Blueberry Vinaigrette

Total **30 min**; Makes ½ **cup**

¼ **cup blueberries**

1 **tsp. sugar**

1 **tsp. fresh lemon juice**

¼ **cup vegetable oil**

1 **Tbsp. balsamic vinegar**

1 **tsp. adobo sauce from a can
of chipotles in adobo sauce**

Salt and pepper

**Baby spinach and quartered
radishes, for serving**

1. In a small saucepan, mash the blueberries with the sugar and lemon juice and bring to a simmer over moderate heat. Cook, stirring, until thickened, about 8 minutes. Let cool slightly.

2. Scrape the blueberry mixture into a medium bowl and whisk in the oil, vinegar and adobo sauce. Season with salt and pepper and serve over baby spinach and radishes.

Make Ahead The vinaigrette can be refrigerated overnight.

Maraschino Blueberries

Active **20 min**; Total **2 days**
Makes **3½ cups**

- 1 tsp. kosher salt
- 2 cups warm water
- 2 cups blueberries
- 2 cups sugar
- 1 cup Chambord liqueur
- 1 Tbsp. fresh lemon juice

1. In a medium bowl, stir the salt into the water until dissolved. Stir in the blueberries and refrigerate overnight.

2. In a medium saucepan, bring the sugar, Chambord and lemon juice to a simmer over high heat, stirring to dissolve the sugar; remove from the heat. Drain and rinse the blueberries and add them to the saucepan. Transfer the blueberries and syrup to a jar and refrigerate for at least 24 hours before serving.

Serve With Ice cream or pancakes, or in cocktails like Manhattans and old-fashioneds.

Flash-Roasted Broccoli with Spicy Crumbs

Total **30 min**; Serves **6**

- 2 oz. sliced pepperoni
- 1 garlic clove, sliced
- 1 cup panko
- ¼ cup plus 2 Tbsp. extra-virgin olive oil
- 2 lbs. broccoli, trimmed and cut into long spears

  Salt
- 2 Tbsp. Dijon mustard

1. Preheat the oven to 425°. In a mini food processor, pulse the pepperoni with the garlic until finely chopped. Add the panko and pulse just to combine.

2. In a medium skillet, heat 2 tablespoons of the olive oil. Add the crumb mixture and cook over moderate heat, stirring, until crisp and golden, about 5 minutes. Scrape onto a plate and let cool.

3. Meanwhile, in a medium bowl, toss the broccoli with the remaining ¼ cup of olive oil and season with salt. Arrange the broccoli on a baking sheet and roast for about 15 minutes, turning once, until tender and browned in spots. Spread the mustard on one side of the broccoli and press the broccoli into the crumbs. Transfer the broccoli to a platter, sprinkle with any remaining crumbs and serve.

Creamy Roasted Broccoli Soup

Active **20 min**; Total **1 hr**
Serves **6**

- 5 unpeeled garlic cloves
- 2 lbs. broccoli, cut into 1-inch florets, stems reserved for another use
- 2 Tbsp. extra-virgin olive oil
- 2 Tbsp. unsalted butter, melted

  Salt and pepper
- 4 oz. cream cheese
- 3 cups low-sodium chicken broth

  Croutons, for serving

1. Preheat the oven to 400°. Wrap the garlic in a foil packet and roast for 50 minutes, until softened. Meanwhile, in a small roasting pan, toss the broccoli with the olive oil and butter and season with salt and pepper. Roast for 20 minutes, until tender.

2. Squeeze the garlic cloves from their skins into a blender. Add the roasted broccoli, cream cheese and chicken broth and puree until smooth. Transfer the soup to a saucepan and bring to a simmer. Season with salt and pepper and serve with croutons.

Make Ahead The soup can be refrigerated overnight. Reheat gently before serving.

Flash-Roasted Broccoli with Spicy Crumbs

Creamy Roasted Broccoli Soup

Broccoli Cheese Dunk, p. 48

Broccoli-Anchovy Fettuccine, p. 48

Broccoli Cheese Dunk

Total **30 min**; Serves **6**

 3 Tbsp. extra-virgin olive oil

1½ lbs. broccoli, cut into 1-inch
   florets, stems peeled and diced

 1 large garlic clove, minced

 1 tsp. ground coriander

 1 tsp. chili powder

 1 tsp. ground cumin

 ½ tsp. dried oregano

   Salt

 1 lb. sliced provolone cheese

   Warm tortillas, for serving

1. Preheat the broiler and position a rack 8 inches from the heat. In a large skillet, heat the olive oil. Add the broccoli and garlic and cook over moderate heat, stirring occasionally, until the broccoli is browned in spots and crisp-tender, about 5 minutes. Stir in the spices and oregano, season with salt and cook for 1 minute. Add ½ cup of water and cook until the broccoli is tender and the liquid has evaporated, about 3 minutes.

2. Arrange half of the cheese in 6 individual gratin dishes. Top with the broccoli and the remaining cheese. Broil for 5 to 6 minutes, until the cheese is melted and browned. Serve right away, with warm tortillas.

Broccoli-Anchovy Fettuccine

Total **20 min**; Serves **6**

12 oz. fettuccine

 ¼ cup extra-virgin olive oil

   One 2-oz. can anchovy fillets,
   drained and chopped

 4 small garlic cloves, minced

 1 lb. broccoli, cut into small
   florets, stems peeled and
   coarsely shredded

 ¼ cup chopped hot
   Peppadew peppers

 ½ cup freshly grated
   Parmigiano-Reggiano cheese,
   plus more for serving

 ¼ cup chopped flat-leaf parsley

1. In a large pot of salted boiling water, cook the pasta just until al dente. Drain, reserving 1 cup of the cooking water.

2. In a large, deep skillet, heat the olive oil. Add the anchovies and garlic and cook over moderately high heat, stirring, until fragrant, about 1 minute. Add the broccoli florets and stems and cook for 2 minutes, stirring occasionally. Add ½ cup of the reserved pasta water, cover and cook until the broccoli is tender but still bright green, about 2 minutes. Mash the broccoli coarsely.

3. Add the pasta, Peppadews and the ½ cup of Parmigiano to the skillet and toss. Add the remaining ½ cup of pasta water and cook, tossing, until the pasta is coated with a light sauce, about 2 minutes. Stir in the parsley and serve in bowls, passing extra Parmigiano on the side.

Wine Tangy, medium-bodied Sauvignon Blanc.

Warm Kale and Broccoli Stem Salad with Leek Vinaigrette

Total **30 min**; Serves **4 or 5**

- ½ **cup hazelnuts**
- 1 **lb. kale, stems and inner ribs removed, leaves thinly sliced**
- 3 **broccoli stems, peeled and julienned (1 cup)**
- **Salt and pepper**
- ¼ **cup extra-virgin olive oil**
- 2 **leeks, white and tender green parts only, thinly sliced**
- 2 **Tbsp. fresh lemon juice**
- ½ **cup coarsely shredded Pecorino Romano or Manchego cheese**

1. Preheat the oven to 350°. Spread the hazelnuts in a pie plate and toast for about 13 minutes, until the skins blister and the nuts are golden. Transfer to a kitchen towel and let cool. Rub off the skins and chop the nuts.

2. Put the kale and broccoli stems in a serving bowl and season with salt. Using your hands, squeeze the vegetables to soften them slightly.

3. In a medium skillet, heat the olive oil. Add the leeks and cook over moderate heat, stirring, until softened, about 3 minutes. Add the lemon juice and season with salt and pepper. Pour the leek vinaigrette over the kale and broccoli and let stand for 2 minutes. Toss well to coat. Add the cheese and hazelnuts and season with pepper; toss again. Serve right away.

Wine Crisp, minerally northern Italian white.

Thai Brussels Sprout Salad

Total **25 min**; Serves **6**

- ⅓ cup fresh lime juice
- 3 Tbsp. Asian fish sauce
- 3 red Thai chiles, minced
- 1 Tbsp. turbinado sugar
- ¾ lb. brussels sprouts, thinly sliced (about 5 cups)
- 2 Honeycrisp apples, cored and chopped
- 1 cup mixed chopped cilantro and basil

  Salt and pepper

In a large bowl, mix the lime juice with the fish sauce, chiles and sugar until the sugar dissolves. Add the brussels sprouts, apples and herbs and season with salt and pepper. Toss to coat, then serve.

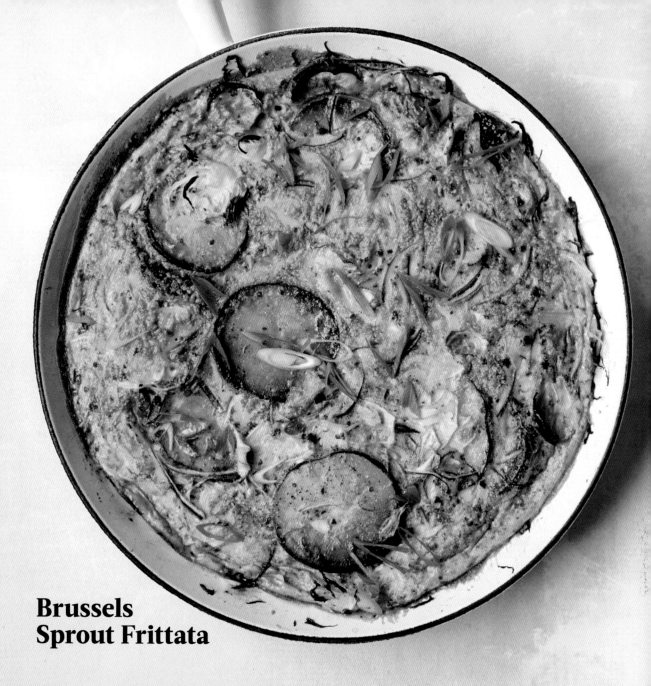

Brussels Sprout Frittata

Total **30 min**; Serves **6**

2 Tbsp. extra-virgin olive oil

½ lb. brussels sprouts, thinly sliced (about 3 cups)

1 small baking potato, peeled and sliced ¼ inch thick

1 small red onion, halved and thinly sliced

Salt and pepper

10 large eggs, beaten

1 tsp. smoked paprika

Thinly sliced scallions, for garnish

Hot sauce, for serving

Preheat the oven to 375°. In a large ovenproof nonstick skillet, heat the olive oil. Add the brussels sprouts, potato and onion and season with salt and pepper. Cover and cook over moderate heat, stirring occasionally, until the vegetables are golden and tender, about 10 minutes. Stir in the eggs and paprika and transfer to the oven. Bake for 10 minutes, until set. Garnish with scallions and serve with hot sauce.

Whole Roast Chicken
with 40 Brussels Sprouts

Whole Roast Chicken with 40 Brussels Sprouts

Active **10 min**; Total **1 hr 15 min**
Serves **4**

One 4-lb. chicken

2 **Tbsp. extra-virgin olive oil**

Salt and pepper

40 **brussels sprouts (1½ lbs.), trimmed**

2 **Tbsp. unsalted butter, cubed**

1 **tsp. caraway seeds**

2 **Tbsp. fresh lemon juice, plus lemon wedges for serving**

Preheat the oven to 450°. Rub the chicken with the olive oil and season with salt and pepper. Place the chicken in a roasting pan and roast for 30 minutes. Add the brussels sprouts, butter and caraway seeds to the pan and roast for 20 minutes longer, until the chicken is cooked through. Sprinkle the lemon juice over the sprouts and let the chicken rest for 15 minutes. Carve the chicken, toss the brussels sprouts and serve with lemon wedges.

Wine Lightly oaked Chardonnay, such as Chablis.

Spaghetti with Brussels Sprout and Sausage Breadcrumbs

Total **20 min**; Serves **2**

½ **lb. spaghetti**

¼ **cup extra-virgin olive oil, plus more for drizzling**

½ **lb. brussels sprouts, thinly sliced (about 3 cups)**

½ **lb. loose pork sausage**

1 **cup panko**

2 **Tbsp. snipped chives**

Salt and pepper

Lemon wedges, for serving

1. In a large pot of salted boiling water, cook the spaghetti until it is al dente.

2. Meanwhile, in a large nonstick skillet, heat the ¼ cup of olive oil. Add the brussels sprouts and sausage and cook over moderately high heat, stirring, until the sausage is browned and cooked through, about 5 minutes. Stir in the panko and cook until crisp, 3 minutes. Stir in the chives and season with salt and pepper.

3. Drain the spaghetti and transfer to a bowl. Top with the brussel sprout breadcrumbs, drizzle with olive oil and serve with lemon wedges.

Wine Juicy, light-bodied Italian red, such as Dolcetto.

Chipotle–Butternut Squash Soup with Chive Cream

Active **30 min**; Total **1 hr**; Serves **8**

- 2 **Tbsp. unsalted butter**
- 1 **medium onion, finely chopped**

  One 3-lb. butternut squash, peeled and diced (8 cups)
- 1 **small canned chipotle in adobo, chopped**
- 7 **cups chicken or turkey stock or low-sodium broth**
- 2 **Tbsp. honey**

  Salt
- 1 **cup crème fraîche**
- ¼ **cup finely chopped chives, plus more for garnish**

1. In a large pot, melt the butter. Add the onion and cook over moderate heat until softened, about 5 minutes. Stir in the squash and chipotle and cook for 1 minute. Add the stock and honey and bring to a boil. Simmer until the squash is tender, about 30 minutes.

2. Transfer the soup to a blender or food processor and puree until smooth. Season with salt.

3. In a small microwave-safe bowl, stir the crème fraîche with the ¼ cup of chives. Microwave until just melted, about 30 seconds. Serve the soup with a swirl of the chive cream and a sprinkling of chives.

Butternut Squash, Apple and Chicken Pan Roast

Active **20 min**; Total **1 hr 40 min**
Serves **6**

- One 1½-lb. butternut squash, peeled and cut into ¾-inch dice
- 3 Fuji apples, peeled and cut into ¾-inch dice
- 1 Tbsp. chopped sage
- ¼ cup extra-virgin olive oil
- Salt and pepper
- 6 whole chicken legs (3 lbs.)
- 2 Tbsp. unsalted butter, thinly sliced

1. Preheat the oven to 400°. In a large roasting pan, toss the squash, apples and sage with the olive oil and season with salt and pepper. Season the chicken legs with salt and pepper and set them on top. Dot with the butter and roast for about 1 hour and 15 minutes, until the squash and apples are tender and the chicken is browned and cooked through.

2. Transfer the chicken to a plate and keep warm. Place the roasting pan over a burner and boil, stirring, until the pan juices are reduced, about 5 minutes. Return the chicken to the pan and serve.

Wine Spiced, ripe pear–scented California Chardonnay.

Squash Rösti Cakes with Sour Cream and Salmon Caviar

Total **45 min**
Makes **4 dozen mini cakes**

One 1-lb. butternut squash neck, peeled and coarsely shredded in a food processor

1½ **lbs. baking potatoes, peeled and coarsely shredded in a food processor**

½ **cup cornstarch**

2 **large eggs**

½ **cup minced onion**

Salt and cayenne

Vegetable oil, for frying

Sour cream, salmon caviar and chives, for garnish

1. In a large bowl, combine the squash and potatoes with the cornstarch, eggs and onion; season with salt and cayenne.

2. In a large nonstick skillet, heat ⅛ inch of oil until shimmering. Add 2-tablespoon-size mounds of the squash mixture and cook over moderate heat, turning once, until golden and cooked through, 4 to 5 minutes. Drain on paper towels and repeat, adding more oil to the skillet as needed and wiping out the pan occasionally.

3. Top the rösti cakes with sour cream, caviar and chives and serve hot.

Wine Rich, slightly nutty Champagne.

Mashed Butternut Squash with Roasted Garlic

Active **30 min**; Total **2 hr**
Serves **6**

Two 2-lb. butternut squash, peeled and sliced ¾ inch thick

12 **garlic cloves, peeled**

¼ **cup extra-virgin olive oil**

1 **rosemary sprig**

1 **jalapeño, halved and seeded**

Salt and pepper

2 **Tbsp. unsalted butter, melted**

1. Preheat the oven to 400°. In a large bowl, toss the squash with the garlic, olive oil, rosemary and jalapeño and season with salt and pepper. Spread the squash mixture on a large baking sheet, cover with foil and roast for about 45 minutes, until tender. Uncover and roast until lightly browned in spots, about 45 minutes longer.

2. Discard the rosemary and mince the jalapeño. Transfer the squash, jalapeño and garlic to a medium bowl. Add the butter, season with salt and pepper and mash coarsely. Serve right away.

Make Ahead The mashed squash can be refrigerated for up to 2 days.

Apricot-Glazed Butternut Squash Tart

Active **45 min**; Total **2 hr**; Serves **8**

- One 1-lb. butternut squash neck–peeled, halved lengthwise and sliced ¼ inch thick
- 2 Tbsp. unsalted butter, melted
- 2 Tbsp. sugar
- 8 oz. all-butter puff pastry, chilled
- 4 oz. cream cheese, softened
- ⅛ tsp. cinnamon
- 2 Tbsp. apricot preserves, melted
- 2 Tbsp. chopped toasted pecans

1. Preheat the oven to 375°. Line a baking sheet with parchment paper and butter the paper. Brush the squash with the melted butter and sprinkle with 1½ tablespoons of the sugar. Roast for about 45 minutes, flipping the squash slices halfway through, until softened. Let cool.

2. Meanwhile, roll out the pastry to a 14-by-6-inch rectangle and transfer it to a parchment paper–lined baking sheet. Prick the pastry all over with a fork and refrigerate until firm, about 5 minutes. Top with another sheet of parchment paper and a flat cookie sheet and bake for about 30 minutes, until the pastry is lightly golden on the bottom but not set. Remove the top cookie sheet and parchment and bake for 10 minutes longer, until the pastry is golden and crisp. Let cool.

3. Blend the cream cheese with the cinnamon and the remaining ½ tablespoon of sugar and spread it on the pastry. Arrange the squash slices on top. Brush with the apricot preserves and sprinkle with pecans. Cut into slices and serve.

Cabbage

61   Cabbage Slaw

61   Fresh Cabbage Kimchi

62   Chicken-Cabbage Salad

62   Potted Ham with Cabbage and Pickles

63   Apple Cider–Braised Cabbage

Canned Tuna

64   Tuna Banh Mi

65   Tuscan White Bean and Escarole Soup with Tuna

66   Tuna Escabeche Tostadas

66   Lemony Tuna and Artichoke Dip

Carrots

69   Curry-Roasted Carrots with Carrot Top Gremolata

69   Nutty Carrot Pilaf

70   Crunchy Carrot and Beet Salad with Herbs

70   Carrot, Coconut and Zucchini Bread

71   Carrot-Pear Shrub

Cauliflower

73   Cauliflower Puree with Horseradish and Caraway

73   Silky Cauliflower Soup with Charmoula and Almonds

74   Stir-Fried Cauliflower "Rice"

74   Faux Tso's Cauliflower

Cherries

76   Israeli Couscous with Cherries and Olives

77   Cherry Hand Pies

78   Cherry-Lime Pudding Cups

78   Pork and Sausage Meat Loaf with Cherries

Chicken

81   Chicken Caesar Skewers

81   Sesame-Ginger Chicken Meatballs

82   Chicken Roasted on Bread with Caperberries

82   Chicken-Chile Soup

83   Lemon-Shallot-Marinated Chicken

83   Honey Mustard Chicken

Chickpeas

84   Chickpea Salad Sandwiches

85   Chickpea and Chard Chili

86   Kale Caesar with Fried Chickpeas

87   Spanish-Style Chickpea Quesadillas

Corn

88   Skillet Corn with Bulgur

88   Corn-Shrimp Dumplings

91   Thai Glazed Corn

91   Parmesan Corn Butter

Cucumbers

92   Cucumber Gazpacho with Shrimp

93   Cucumber and Sugar Snap Salad with Nutty Granola

93   Cucumber and Salami Fried Rice with Arugula

94   Grilled Marinated Cucumbers and Eggplant

94   Dill Pickles

Cabbage Slaw

Fresh Cabbage Kimchi

Chicken–Cabbage Salad, p. 62

Potted Ham with Cabbage and Pickles, p. 62

Cabbage Slaw

Total **30 min**; Serves **6**

1 white or pink grapefruit
   or 2 Oroblanco

2 mandarin oranges
   or clementines

4 kumquats, thinly sliced

½ lb. brussels sprouts or Savoy
   cabbage, finely shredded

⅓ cup pitted green olives,
   chopped

4 Medjool dates, pitted and
   thinly sliced

3 Tbsp. extra-virgin olive oil

   Salt and pepper

Using a sharp knife, peel the grapefruit and mandarin oranges, removing all of the bitter white pith. Working over a large bowl, cut in between the membranes and release the sections into the bowl. Squeeze the juice from the grapefruit membranes into the bowl; you will need ¼ cup. Add the kumquats, brussels sprouts or cabbage, olives, dates and olive oil and season with salt and pepper. Toss and serve.

Fresh Cabbage Kimchi

Active **15 min**; Total **1 hr 15 min**
Makes **6 cups**

1 lb. napa cabbage, chopped

1 lb. baby bok choy, trimmed and
   quartered lengthwise

⅓ cup kosher salt

¼ cup plus 1 tsp. sugar

2 Tbsp. Asian fish sauce

1 heaping Tbsp. Korean
   red pepper flakes (gochugaru)
   or 1 tsp. crushed red pepper

2 tsp. finely grated or minced garlic

1 tsp. finely grated peeled
   fresh ginger

1 Tbsp. toasted sesame oil,
   plus more for drizzling

   Toasted sesame seeds,
   for garnish

1. In a large bowl, combine the napa cabbage and bok choy. In a large saucepan, combine the salt and ¼ cup of the sugar with 2 quarts of water and warm over moderate heat just until the salt and sugar dissolve. Pour the brine over the cabbages and let stand at room temperature for 30 minutes.

2. Rinse and drain the cabbages and return them to the bowl. Add the fish sauce, red pepper flakes, garlic, ginger, 1 tablespoon of sesame oil and the remaining 1 teaspoon of sugar; toss well. Let stand for 30 minutes. Drizzle the kimchi with sesame oil and garnish with sesame seeds before serving.

Chicken-Cabbage Salad

Total **20 min**; Serves **4**

- **5 Tbsp. canola oil**
- **3 Tbsp. fresh lime juice**
- **1½ Tbsp. Asian fish sauce**
- **1 Thai chile or ½ serrano chile, minced**
- **Salt and pepper**
- **6 cups mixed finely shredded Savoy cabbage and red cabbage**
- **2 small carrots, finely shredded**
- **Meat from ½ cooked chicken, shredded (2 cups)**
- **One 2-oz. package ramen, noodles crushed, seasoning packet reserved for another use**
- **½ cup mixed chopped basil and cilantro**

In a large bowl, whisk the canola oil with the lime juice, fish sauce and chile; season with salt and pepper. Add both cabbages, the carrots, chicken, noodles and herbs, toss and serve.

Wine Lime-scented, dry Australian Riesling.

Potted Ham with Cabbage and Pickles

Total **20 min**; Makes **2 cups**

- **2 oil-packed anchovy fillets**
- **¼ cup extra-virgin olive oil**
- **½ lb. smoked ham, shredded**
- **1 cup finely chopped green cabbage**
- **1 small dill pickle, chopped (⅓ cup)**
- **2 Tbsp. chopped dill, plus more for garnish**
- **Salt and pepper**
- **Toasted country bread and mustard, for serving**

In a small saucepan, melt the anchovies in the olive oil over moderate heat, stirring. Scrape the anchovy oil into a medium bowl. Add the ham, cabbage, pickle and 2 tablespoons of chopped dill; season with salt and pepper and mix well. Pack the ham mixture into a 3-cup ramekin and garnish with more chopped dill. Serve at room temperature with bread and mustard.

Make Ahead The potted ham can be refrigerated for up to 2 days.

Wine Fragrant, berried dry rosé.

Apple Cider–Braised Cabbage

Active **30 min**; Total **1 hr**
Serves **4 to 6**

2 Tbsp. extra-virgin olive oil

One 1½-lb. head of green cabbage, cut through the core into 6 wedges

2 oz. bacon, chopped (½ cup)

1 medium onion, halved through the core and thinly sliced lengthwise

Salt

½ cup apple cider vinegar

2 cups apple cider

1 Tbsp. unsalted butter

Pepper

1. In a large, deep skillet, heat the olive oil until shimmering. Add the cabbage wedges cut side down and cook over moderate heat, turning once, until browned, 6 to 8 minutes. Transfer to a plate.

2. Add the bacon to the skillet and cook over moderate heat, stirring occasionally, until rendered but not crisp, about 5 minutes. Add the onion and a generous pinch of salt and cook, stirring occasionally, until softened and just starting to brown, about 10 minutes. Stir in the vinegar and simmer over moderately high heat until reduced by half, about 3 minutes. Add the cider and bring to a boil. Nestle the cabbage wedges in the skillet, cover and braise over moderately low heat, turning once, until tender, about 20 minutes. Using a slotted spoon or spatula, transfer the cabbage to a platter and tent with foil.

3. Boil the sauce over moderately high heat, stirring occasionally, until slightly thickened, about 5 minutes. Remove the skillet from the heat, swirl in the butter and season with salt and pepper. Spoon the sauce over the braised cabbage and serve.

Serve With Seared scallops or roast fish.

Make Ahead The cabbage can be prepared through Step 2 and refrigerated overnight in the braising liquid. Let return to room temperature before finishing.

Tuna Banh Mi

Total **20 min**; Serves **4**

15 oz. tuna in olive oil, drained

¼ cup fresh lime juice

 2 Tbsp. Asian fish sauce

 1 jalapeño, minced

    Salt and pepper

    One 24- to 32-inch soft baguette, split and toasted

    Mayonnaise, mint leaves, julienned carrots and sliced dill pickles, for serving

In a medium bowl, toss the tuna with the lime juice, fish sauce and jalapeño. Season with salt and pepper. Spread the cut sides of the baguette with mayonnaise and fill with the tuna salad, mint, carrots and pickles. Close, cut into 4 sandwiches and serve.

Beer Fresh, grassy pale ale.

Tuscan White Bean and Escarole Soup with Tuna

Total **30 min**; Serves **4**

- ¼ **cup extra-virgin olive oil**
- 1 **onion, chopped**
- 3 **garlic cloves, chopped**
- 10 **oz. escarole, chopped**
- 2 **tsp. finely chopped rosemary**
- 6 **cups chicken stock or low-sodium broth**
- **One 15-oz. can cannellini beans, rinsed**
- 15 **oz. tuna in olive oil, drained**
- **Salt and pepper**
- **Shaved Parmesan cheese and crusty bread, for serving**

Heat the oil in a pot. Add the onion and garlic and cook over moderate heat, stirring occasionally, until softened and just starting to brown, about 10 minutes. Add the escarole and rosemary and cook until the escarole is wilted, about 3 minutes. Add the stock, beans and tuna and bring to a boil. Simmer over low heat for 5 minutes. Season with salt and pepper. Serve the soup with shaved Parmesan and crusty bread.

Tuna Escabeche Tostadas

Total **30 min**; Serves **4 to 6**

Canola oil, for frying

6 corn tortillas (see Note)

Salt

15 oz. tuna in olive oil, drained

¼ cup chopped pickled Mexican jalapeños and carrots from a can, plus ¼ cup of the brine

Cilantro leaves, sliced radishes and toasted pumpkin seeds, for serving

1. In a medium skillet, heat ¼ inch of oil until shimmering. Add 1 tortilla to the hot oil and fry over moderate heat, turning, until browned and crisp, 2 to 3 minutes. Transfer to paper towels to drain and season the tostada lightly with salt. Repeat with the remaining tortillas.

2. In a medium bowl, mix the tuna with the jalapeños and carrots and their brine. Spoon the tuna escabeche onto the tostadas and top with cilantro, radishes and toasted pumpkin seeds. Serve right away.

Note You can use store-bought tostadas instead of frying tortillas at home.

Beer Lightly hoppy, crisp lager.

Lemony Tuna and Artichoke Dip

Total **30 min**; Serves **4 to 6**

10 oz. frozen artichoke quarters, thawed and patted dry

7½ oz. tuna in olive oil, drained

¾ cup mayonnaise

2 tsp. fresh lemon juice

1 tsp. hot sauce

1 garlic clove, finely grated

¼ cup freshly grated Parmigiano-Reggiano cheese

Salt and pepper

Crudités and chips, for serving

Preheat the oven to 375°. In a medium bowl, mix the artichokes with the tuna, mayonnaise, lemon juice, hot sauce, garlic and Parmesan. Season the dip with salt and pepper and scrape into a small ovenproof skillet. Bake for 15 minutes, until hot. Turn on the broiler and broil 8 inches from the heat until browned, 1 to 2 minutes. Serve with crudités and chips.

Make Ahead The unbaked dip can be refrigerated overnight. Let stand at room temperature for 30 minutes before baking.

Wine Bright, green apple–scented cava.

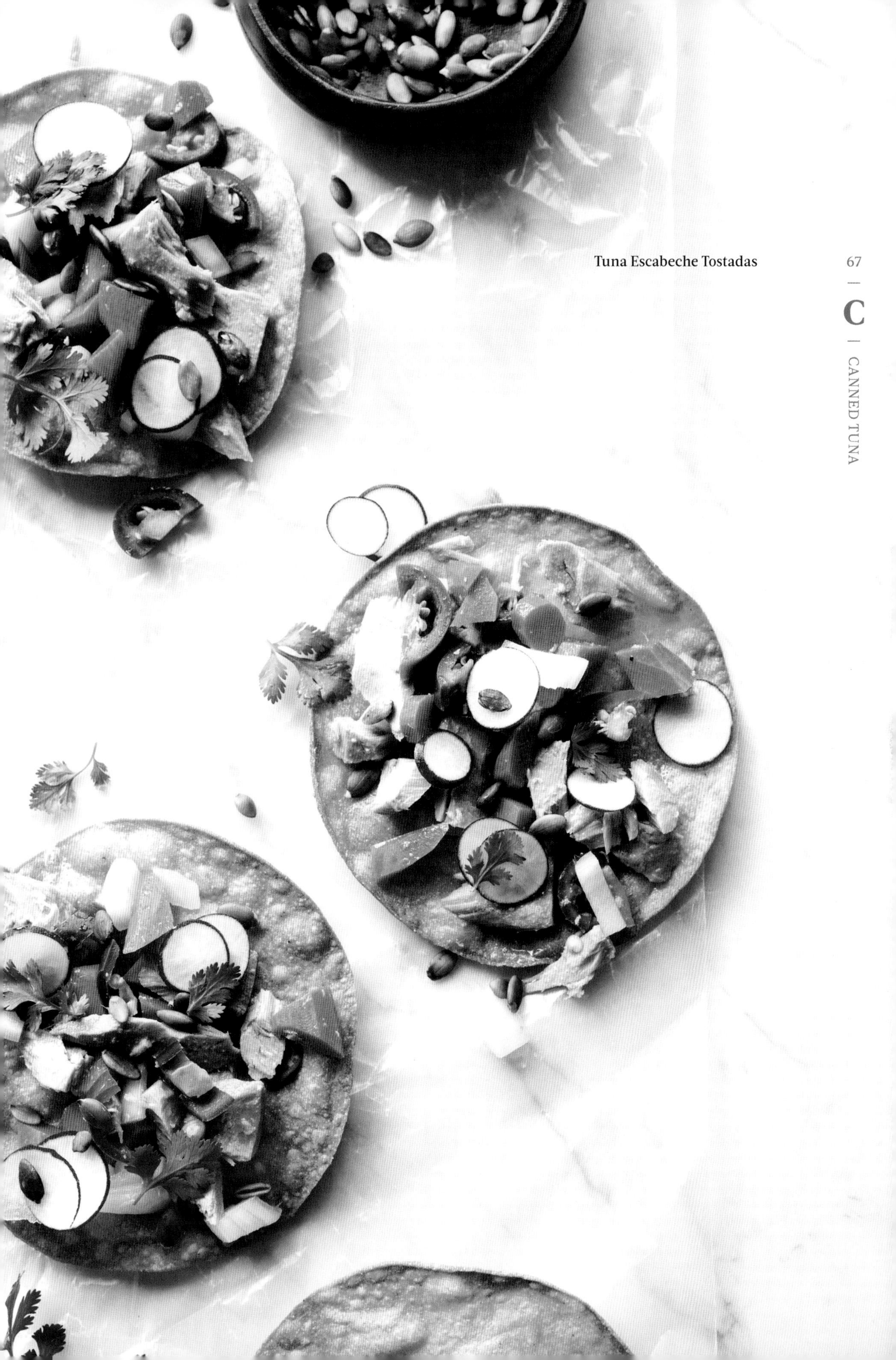

Tuna Escabeche Tostadas

Curry-Roasted Carrots with
Carrot Top Gremolata

Nutty Carrot Pilaf

Crunchy Carrot and Beet Salad
with Herbs, p. 70

Carrot, Coconut and Zucchini Bread, p. 70

Curry-Roasted Carrots with Carrot Top Gremolata

Total **40 min**; Serves **4 to 6**

3 **bunches of small carrots with tops (2 lbs.), scrubbed, tops reserved**

2 **large shallots, thinly sliced**

3 **Tbsp. extra-virgin olive oil**

2 **tsp. curry powder**

Salt and pepper

2 **Tbsp. fresh lemon juice**

¼ **cup chopped cilantro**

1 **tsp. finely grated lemon zest**

½ **jalapeño, minced**

1. Preheat the oven to 425°. On a baking sheet, toss the carrots and shallots with the olive oil and curry powder and season with salt and pepper. Roast for 20 to 25 minutes, stirring occasionally, until the carrots are tender and golden. Drizzle with the lemon juice, toss to coat and transfer to a platter.

2. Meanwhile, in a small bowl, combine the cilantro, lemon zest and jalapeño. Finely chop the carrot tops until you have ½ cup and add them to the bowl.

3. Sprinkle the carrot top gremolata over the carrots and shallots and serve.

Nutty Carrot Pilaf

Active **15 min**; Total **45 min** Serves **6 to 8**

2 **Tbsp. extra-virgin olive oil**

3 **medium carrots, cut into ½-inch pieces (2 cups)**

1 **shallot, finely chopped**

Salt and pepper

1½ **cups basmati rice**

¾ **tsp. caraway seeds**

¼ **cup chopped parsley**

⅓ **cup salted roasted pepitas (hulled pumpkin seeds)**

⅓ **cup chopped roasted almonds**

Lemon wedges, for serving

1. In a large saucepan, heat the olive oil over moderately high heat. Add the carrots and shallot, season with salt and pepper and cook, stirring occasionally, until the shallot is softened, about 3 minutes. Stir in the rice and caraway seeds. Add 2½ cups of water and bring to a boil. Cover and cook over low heat until the rice is tender and the water is absorbed, about 15 minutes. Remove from the heat and let stand, covered, for 10 minutes.

2. Fluff the rice with a fork. Stir in the parsley and season with salt and pepper. Transfer the pilaf to a bowl and sprinkle with the pepitas and almonds. Serve with lemon wedges.

Crunchy Carrot and Beet Salad with Herbs

Total **30 min**; Serves **4 to 6**

- ¼ **cup extra-virgin olive oil, plus more for drizzling**
- ¼ **cup fresh lemon juice**
- ½ **cup chopped mixed herbs, such as chives and parsley**

  Salt and coarsely ground pepper
- ½ **lb. carrots, peeled and very thinly sliced, preferably on a mandoline**
- 2 **medium beets, peeled and very thinly sliced, preferably on a mandoline**
- 6 **oz. white button or cremini mushrooms, very thinly sliced**

  Parmigiano-Reggiano shavings, for garnish

1. In a large bowl, whisk the ¼ cup of olive oil with the lemon juice and half of the herbs; season with salt and pepper. Add the carrots and beets, toss to coat and let stand at room temperature for 15 minutes.

2. Arrange the mushrooms on a platter and top with the carrots and beets. Drizzle with olive oil, garnish with Parmigiano-Reggiano and the remaining herbs and serve.

Carrot, Coconut and Zucchini Bread

Active **20 min**; Total **2 hr plus cooling**; Makes **one 8-by-4-inch loaf**

- 2 **cups all-purpose flour**
- ¾ **tsp. kosher salt**
- ½ **tsp. baking powder**
- ½ **tsp. baking soda**
- 2 **large eggs, beaten**
- ½ **cup canola oil**
- ¾ **cup light brown sugar**
- ½ **cup granulated sugar**
- 2 **large carrots, grated on the large holes of a box grater (1 packed cup)**
- 1 **medium zucchini, grated on the large holes of a box grater (1 packed cup)**
- 1¼ **cups shredded sweetened coconut**

1. Preheat the oven to 375°. Spray an 8-by-4-inch loaf pan with cooking spray.

2. In a medium bowl, whisk the flour with the salt, baking powder and baking soda. In a large bowl, whisk the eggs with the canola oil and both sugars until smooth. Stir in the carrots, zucchini and ¾ cup of the shredded coconut, then fold in the dry ingredients just until combined.

3. Scrape the batter into the prepared pan and sprinkle with the remaining ½ cup of coconut. Loosely tent the pan with foil and bake for about 1½ hours, until the top is golden brown and a tester inserted in the center of the loaf comes out clean. Transfer the bread to a rack to cool for 30 minutes, then turn it out and let cool completely.

Make Ahead The bread can be wrapped and kept at room temperature for up to 2 days.

Carrot-Pear Shrub

Total **15 min**; Makes **2 drinks**

1 **lb. carrots, peeled and grated on the large holes of a box grater (3 packed cups)**

2 **ripe Anjou pears–peeled, cored and chopped (2 cups)**

2 **Tbsp. finely grated peeled fresh ginger**

3 **Tbsp. fresh lime juice**

1 **Tbsp. raw unfiltered apple cider vinegar**

½ **tsp. kosher salt**

Ice, for serving

In a blender, combine all of the ingredients except the ice with ½ cup of water and puree until smooth. Strain the shrub through a sieve lined with 3 layers of cheesecloth, pressing on the solids. Serve in 2 glasses over ice.

Cauliflower Puree
with Horseradish
and Caraway

Cauliflower Puree with Horseradish and Caraway

Total **20 min**; Serves **4**

1³/₄ lbs. cauliflower, cored and cut into florets

6 Tbsp. butter, plus more for serving

3 Tbsp. prepared horseradish, drained

Salt and pepper

Caraway seeds, for garnish

Set a steamer basket in a large saucepan filled with 1 inch of water. Add the cauliflower, cover and steam over high heat until tender, about 10 minutes. Transfer to a food processor and puree with the 6 tablespoons of butter and the horseradish. Season with salt and pepper. Transfer the puree to a serving bowl, garnish with caraway seeds and serve with butter.

Make Ahead The cauliflower puree can be refrigerated for up to 2 days. Reheat gently before serving.

Silky Cauliflower Soup with Charmoula and Smoked Almonds

Total **30 min**; Serves **4**

1³/₄ lbs. cauliflower, cored and cut into florets

Salt and pepper

¹/₂ cup extra-virgin olive oil

3 Tbsp. fresh lemon juice

¹/₄ cup minced parsley

1 garlic clove, minced

1 tsp. ground coriander

Crushed smoked almonds, for garnish

1. In a large saucepan, cover the cauliflower with 6 cups of water and bring to a boil. Simmer over moderate heat until the cauliflower is very soft, about 10 minutes. Transfer to a blender and puree until very smooth. Season the soup with salt and pepper.

2. In a medium bowl, whisk the olive oil with the lemon juice, parsley, garlic and coriander; season with salt and pepper. Ladle the soup into bowls and drizzle some of the charmoula on top. Garnish with crushed almonds and serve.

Make Ahead The soup and charmoula can be refrigerated separately overnight. Let the charmoula come to room temperature and reheat the soup gently before serving.

Stir-Fried Cauliflower "Rice"

Total **35 min**; Serves **4**

1³⁄₄ **lbs. cauliflower, cored and cut into 1¹⁄₂-inch florets**

¹⁄₃ **cup canola oil**

3 **Tbsp. minced peeled fresh ginger**

3 **Tbsp. minced garlic**

1 **cup chopped cilantro, plus more for garnish**

2 **fresh hot red chiles, thinly sliced**

3 **Tbsp. soy sauce**

2 **Tbsp. fresh lime juice**

Salt

In a food processor, pulse the cauliflower until finely chopped. In a large skillet, heat the oil until shimmering. Add the ginger and garlic and stir-fry over high heat until fragrant, about 1 minute. Add the cauliflower and stir-fry until crisp-tender, about 4 minutes. Stir in the 1 cup of cilantro and the red chiles, soy sauce and lime juice. Season with salt, garnish with chopped cilantro and serve.

Faux Tso's Cauliflower

Total **30 min**; Serves **4**

¹⁄₂ **cup chicken stock or low-sodium broth**

3 **Tbsp. soy sauce**

1 **Tbsp. rice vinegar**

1 **Tbsp. sambal oelek**

1 **Tbsp. cornstarch**

¹⁄₄ **cup canola oil**

1¹⁄₄ **lbs. cauliflower, cored and cut into ³⁄₄-inch florets**

Thinly sliced scallions and sesame seeds, for garnish

Steamed rice, for serving

1. In a small bowl, whisk the chicken stock with the soy sauce, rice vinegar, sambal oelek and cornstarch.

2. In a large skillet, heat the oil until shimmering. Add the cauliflower and cook over moderate heat, stirring occasionally, until tender and browned, 10 to 12 minutes. Stir in the sauce and cook, stirring occasionally, until thickened, about 4 minutes. Garnish with scallions and sesame seeds and serve with steamed rice.

Wine Tropical fruit–scented South African Chenin Blanc.

Faux Tso's
Cauliflower

Israeli Couscous with Cherries and Olives

Total **25 min**; Serves **4**

- **3 Tbsp. extra-virgin olive oil**
- **1½ cups Israeli couscous**
- **1½ cups cherries, pitted and coarsely chopped**
- **½ cup oil-cured black olives, pitted and chopped**
- **¼ cup chopped tarragon**
- **1 Tbsp. fresh lemon juice**
- **Salt and pepper**

1. In a medium saucepan, heat 1 tablespoon of the olive oil. Add the couscous and cook over moderate heat, stirring, until lightly golden, about 3 minutes. Add 2 cups of water, cover and cook over low heat until the couscous is tender and all of the liquid is absorbed, about 10 minutes.

2. Transfer the couscous to a bowl and stir in the cherries, olives, tarragon, lemon juice and the remaining 2 tablespoons of olive oil. Season with salt and pepper and serve.

Cherry Hand Pies

Active **25 min**; Total **1 hr**; Serves **8**

> One 14-oz. package all-butter puff pastry, thawed and chilled
>
> 2 cups cherries, pitted and coarsely chopped
>
> ¼ cup sugar
>
> 1 Tbsp. cornstarch
>
> 1 Tbsp. fresh lemon juice
>
> ⅛ tsp. cinnamon
>
> 1 large egg, beaten

1. Preheat the oven to 350°. Using a lightly floured rolling pin, roll out the puff pastry on parchment paper to a 14-by-12-inch rectangle, then cut into eight 6-by-3½-inch pieces. Transfer the pastry and parchment to a baking sheet.

2. In a medium bowl, toss the cherries with the sugar, cornstarch, lemon juice and cinnamon. Brush the edges of the pastry rectangles with some of the beaten egg. Mound the filling in the center of each pastry and fold the dough over; press to seal and crimp decoratively. Brush the pies with beaten egg and make a small slit in the top of each one. Bake for 40 minutes, until golden. Let cool slightly before serving.

Cherry-Lime Buttermilk Pudding Cups

Total **15 min plus overnight setting**
Serves **6**

One ¼-oz. package
unflavored powdered gelatin

1 cup buttermilk

2 cups whole milk

½ cup honey

1 Tbsp. fresh lime juice

1½ cups cherries, pitted and
coarsely chopped

2 tsp. finely grated lime zest,
for garnish

1. In a small bowl, whisk the gelatin with ⅓ cup of the buttermilk. Let stand for 5 minutes.

2. In a small saucepan, combine the milk and honey and warm over low heat, stirring, just until the honey dissolves. Remove from the heat and whisk in the gelatin mixture until dissolved. Whisk in the lime juice and the remaining ⅔ cup of buttermilk. Pour the pudding into six 6-ounce cups or ramekins. Cover and chill overnight, until set and firm. Garnish with the cherries and lime zest and serve.

Pork and Sausage Meat Loaf with Cherries

Active **25 min**; Total **1 hr 15 min**
Makes **one 12-by-4-inch loaf**

12 saltine crackers, finely
crushed (about ½ cup)

2 large eggs, beaten

1½ lbs. ground pork

½ lb. loose breakfast sausage,
crumbled

1½ cups cherries, pitted and
coarsely chopped

1 tsp. kosher salt

½ tsp. pepper

¼ cup Dijon mustard

Chopped parsley, for garnish

1. Preheat the oven to 375°. Line a baking sheet with parchment paper.

2. In a large bowl, combine the saltines, eggs, pork, sausage, cherries, salt, pepper and ½ cup of water. Mix gently. Transfer the meat to the baking sheet and form it into a 12-by-4-inch oval loaf. Bake for about 50 minutes, until browned and cooked through. Spread the mustard on top, sprinkle with parsley and serve.

Wine Lively, cherry-scented Italian red, such as Barbera.

Cherry-Lime
Buttermilk
Pudding Cups

Chicken Caesar Skewers

Sesame-Ginger Chicken Meatballs

Chicken Roasted
on Bread, p. 82

Chicken-Chile
Soup, p. 82

Chicken Caesar Skewers

Active **20 min**; Total **50 min**
Serves **4 to 6**

½   **cup mayonnaise**

1   **Tbsp. Dijon mustard**

1   **Tbsp. extra-virgin olive oil**

1   **Tbsp. minced anchovies**

1   **garlic clove, minced**

2   **lbs. boneless, skinless chicken breasts or thighs, cut into 1-inch pieces**

12 **long wooden skewers, soaked in water for 1 hour**

Freshly grated Parmigiano-Reggiano cheese, for garnish

Romaine lettuce and lemon wedges, for serving

1. In a large bowl, whisk the mayonnaise with the mustard, olive oil, anchovies and garlic. Add the chicken and toss to coat. Let marinate at room temperature for 20 minutes.

2. Preheat the broiler and position the rack 6 inches from the heat. Thread the chicken onto the skewers and arrange on a large baking sheet. Broil for 8 to 10 minutes, until lightly browned and cooked through. Transfer the skewers to a platter. Sprinkle with grated Parmigiano-Reggiano and serve with lettuce cups and lemon wedges.

Wine Lemony Sauvignon Blanc, such as Sancerre.

Sesame-Ginger Chicken Meatballs

Total **30 min**; Serves **4**

Canola oil, for brushing

1   **lb. ground chicken, preferably dark meat**

½   **cup plain dry breadcrumbs**

⅓   **cup minced scallions, plus thinly sliced scallions for garnish**

3   **Tbsp. minced peeled fresh ginger**

1   **large egg**

2   **garlic cloves, minced**

2   **tsp. toasted sesame oil**

2   **tsp. soy sauce**

¼   **tsp. kosher salt**

Asian chile sauce, for serving

Preheat the oven to 450° and brush a rimmed baking sheet with canola oil. In a large bowl, mix together all of the remaining ingredients except the sliced scallions and chile sauce. Form the chicken mixture into 1½-inch balls and arrange them on the baking sheet. Brush the meatballs with canola oil and bake for about 13 minutes, until browned and cooked through. Transfer the meatballs to a platter, garnish with sliced scallions and serve with Asian chile sauce.

Wine Brightly fruity, light-bodied Beaujolais.

Chicken Roasted on Bread with Caperberries and Charred Lemons

Active **20 min**; Total **1 hr 10 min**
Serves **4**

½ **lb. sourdough bread,**
   torn into bite-size pieces

4 **large shallots,**
   quartered lengthwise

¾ **cup drained caperberries**

2 **lemons, scrubbed and**
   quartered lengthwise

¼ **cup extra-virgin olive oil,**
   plus more for brushing

   Salt and pepper

   Four 12-oz. whole chicken legs

Preheat the oven to 400°. On a large rimmed baking sheet, toss the bread with the shallots, caperberries, lemons and the ¼ cup of olive oil; season with salt and pepper. Brush the chicken legs with oil and season with salt and pepper. Arrange the chicken on the bread and roast for about 50 minutes, until the bread is crisp and an instant-read thermometer inserted in the thighs registers 160°. Transfer the chicken, bread and vegetables to plates and serve.

Wine Savory, full-bodied white Burgundy.

Chicken-Chile Soup

Total **30 min**; Serves **6 to 8**

3 **Tbsp. extra-virgin olive oil**

2 **poblano chiles–stemmed,**
   seeded and thinly sliced

1 **onion, chopped**

2 **garlic cloves, sliced**

1½ **tsp. ground coriander**

   Salt

2 **quarts chicken stock or**
   low-sodium broth

4 **cups shredded cooked**
   chicken (1¼ lbs.)

   Two 15-oz. cans hominy,
   rinsed and drained

   Chopped cilantro and thinly
   sliced radishes, for garnish

   Lime wedges, for serving

In a large saucepan, heat the olive oil until shimmering. Add the chiles, onion, garlic, coriander and a generous pinch of salt and cook over moderate heat, stirring occasionally, until the chiles are softened, about 8 minutes. Add the stock and bring to a boil. Stir in the chicken and hominy and simmer over moderate heat for 5 minutes. Season with salt. Ladle the soup into shallow bowls, garnish with cilantro and radishes and serve with lime wedges.

Make Ahead The soup can be refrigerated for up to 2 days. Reheat gently before serving.

BONUS RECIPE BY CHEF MICHAEL SYMON

Lemon-Shallot-Marinated Chicken

Active **20 min**; Total **1 hr 30 min**
Serves **4**

- 2 tsp. finely grated
  lemon zest

- ⅓ cup fresh lemon juice

- 2 Tbsp. finely chopped oregano

- 1 small shallot, minced

- 1 garlic clove, minced

- ⅓ cup plus 2 Tbsp.
  extra-virgin olive oil,
  plus more for the grill

- 8 bone-in chicken pieces

  Salt and pepper

1. In a small bowl, whisk the lemon zest and juice with the oregano, shallot, garlic and ⅓ cup plus 2 tablespoons of olive oil. In a large resealable plastic bag, coat the chicken pieces with the marinade and let stand at room temperature for 30 minutes.

2. Light a grill and oil the grate. Scrape the marinade off the chicken and season the pieces with salt and pepper. Grill the chicken over moderate heat, turning occasionally, until lightly charred, white throughout and an instant-read thermometer inserted in a thigh registers 168°, about 40 minutes.

Wine Brisk, lemony Greek white, like Assyrtiko.

BONUS RECIPE BY CHEF BOBBY FLAY

Honey Mustard Chicken

Active **20 min**; Total **1 hr**
Serves **6**

- Two 4-lb. chickens,
  each cut into 8 pieces

- ¼ cup extra-virgin olive oil

  Kosher salt

- 1 cup honey

- 2 Tbsp. Dijon mustard

- 1 tsp. coarsely ground pepper

1. Preheat the oven to 400°. On 2 large rimmed baking sheets, toss the chicken and oil; season with salt. Roast until nearly cooked through, 20 minutes for the breasts and 25 minutes for the legs, thighs and wings. Pour off the fat from the baking sheets. Preheat the broiler; position a rack just below center.

2. In a small saucepan, combine the honey, mustard, pepper and a pinch of salt and bring to a boil.

3. On one of the baking sheets, toss all of the chicken with the honey mixture. Broil skin side down, basting with the honey and shifting the baking sheet as necessary, until browned, about 5 minutes. Turn the chicken skin side up; broil, basting occasionally, until the chicken is cooked through and the skin is deeply glazed but not blackened, 5 minutes longer. Transfer to a platter. Pour the juices from the baking sheet into a heatproof bowl and skim the fat. Serve the chicken, passing the juices on the side.

Wine Rich Zinfandel from California's Amador County.

Chickpea Salad Sandwiches

Total **20 min**; Serves **4**

One 14-oz. can chickpeas, rinsed

2 Tbsp. mayonnaise

2 Tbsp. minced red onion

1 Tbsp. fresh lemon juice

1 Tbsp. chopped dill

Salt and pepper

8 slices of multigrain bread, toasted

Sliced avocado and radish or alfalfa sprouts, for topping

In a large bowl, gently mash the chickpeas with a fork. Stir in the mayonnaise, onion, lemon juice and dill. Season with salt and pepper. Spoon the chickpea salad onto 4 toasts and top with sliced avocado and sprouts. Close the sandwiches and serve.

Chickpea and Swiss Chard Chili

Total **30 min**; Serves **6**

- **6 slices of bacon, chopped**
- **1 large onion, chopped**
- **1 large carrot, cut into ½-inch pieces**
- **2 garlic cloves, thinly sliced**
- **Salt and pepper**
- **One 28-oz. can crushed tomatoes**
- **2 cups chicken stock or low-sodium broth**
- **Two 15-oz. cans chickpeas, rinsed**
- **1 lb. Swiss chard, leaves and stems chopped**
- **3 chipotles in adobo, minced**
- **Shredded Monterey Jack cheese, for serving**

In a large saucepan, cook the bacon over moderately high heat, stirring occasionally, until the fat is rendered, about 7 minutes. Add the onion, carrot, garlic and a generous pinch each of salt and pepper and cook, stirring occasionally, until softened, 8 to 10 minutes. Add the tomatoes, stock, chickpeas, Swiss chard and chipotles and bring to a boil. Simmer over moderately low heat until the chili is thickened and the Swiss chard is wilted and just tender, about 8 minutes. Serve in bowls, topped with shredded cheese.

Make Ahead The chili can be refrigerated overnight. Reheat gently before serving.

Kale Caesar with Fried Chickpeas

Total **45 min**; Serves **4**

> Canola oil, for frying
>
> One 15-oz. can chickpeas, rinsed and patted dry
>
> Salt and pepper
>
> ½ cup mayonnaise
>
> 2 Tbsp. fresh lemon juice
>
> 2 tsp. Dijon mustard
>
> 1 garlic clove, finely grated
>
> ¼ cup shredded Parmesan, plus more for serving
>
> 1¼ lbs. curly kale, stemmed and chopped (10 cups)

1. In a large skillet, heat ¼ inch of oil until shimmering. Add the chickpeas and fry over moderately high heat, stirring occasionally, until browned and crisp, 3 to 5 minutes. Using a slotted spoon, transfer the chickpeas to paper towels to drain. Season with salt and pepper.

2. In a large bowl, whisk the mayonnaise with the lemon juice, mustard, garlic and the ¼ cup of cheese. Season with salt and pepper. Add the kale and toss to coat. Add the fried chickpeas and toss again. Top with shredded Parmesan and serve.

Wine Citrusy, medium-bodied Spanish white, like Verdejo.

Spanish-Style Chickpea Quesadillas

Total **45 min**; Serves **4 to 6**

  One 15-oz. can chickpeas, rinsed

½ lb. Manchego cheese, shredded (2 cups)

 4 piquillo peppers, chopped

¼ cup thinly sliced scallions, plus more for garnish

  Salt and pepper

  Canola oil, for brushing

  Eight 8-inch flour tortillas

  Hot sauce, for serving

1. In a large bowl, mash the chickpeas with a fork. Stir in the cheese, piquillos and ¼ cup of scallions and season with salt and pepper.

2. Heat a large nonstick skillet and brush it with oil. Place 1 tortilla in the skillet and scatter one-fourth of the chickpea mixture evenly on top. Cover with another tortilla and cook over moderately high heat until crisp on the bottom, about 3 minutes. Flip the quesadilla and cook until the cheese is melted, 2 to 3 minutes longer. Transfer the quesadilla to a platter. Repeat with the remaining tortillas and chickpea mixture. Cut the quesadillas into wedges, garnish with sliced scallions and serve with hot sauce.

Make Ahead The chickpea mixture can be refrigerated overnight. Let stand at room temperature for 30 minutes before making the quesadillas.

Beer Light, slightly bitter pilsner.

Skillet Corn with Bulgur

Total **25 min**; Serves **4**

⅓ cup medium-grind bulgur

1 cup chopped tomatoes

1 cup chopped flat-leaf parsley

1 Tbsp. fresh lemon juice

¼ cup extra-virgin olive oil

3 ears of corn, shucked, kernels cut off the cobs

3 garlic cloves, thinly sliced

Salt and pepper

1. In a medium saucepan of boiling water, cook the bulgur until tender, about 15 minutes. Drain very well and transfer to a large bowl. Add the tomatoes, parsley and lemon juice.

2. Meanwhile, in a large skillet, heat the olive oil. Add the corn and garlic and cook over high heat, stirring occasionally, until the corn is charred, about 5 minutes. Scrape the corn into the bowl and season with salt and pepper. Mix well and serve.

Make Ahead The dish can be refrigerated overnight. Serve at room temperature.

Corn-Shrimp Dumplings

Total **30 min**; Makes **20 dumplings**

1 ear of corn, shucked, kernels cut off the cob

½ lb. shelled and deveined shrimp, chopped

2 scallions, minced

2 tsp. minced garlic

2 tsp. minced peeled fresh ginger

Salt

20 small round gyoza wrappers

Soy sauce, for dipping

1. In a medium bowl, mix the corn with the shrimp, scallions, garlic and ginger and season with salt. Brush the edges of the wrappers with water and spoon 1 tablespoon of the filling in the center of each. Fold one side of the wrapper over to form a half-moon, pressing the edges together to seal.

2. In a steamer basket, steam the dumplings over simmering water until cooked through, 3 to 4 minutes. Alternatively, boil the dumplings for about 3 minutes. Serve with soy sauce.

Make Ahead The uncooked dumplings can be frozen for up to 1 month.

Wine Juicy, berry-rich rosé.

Skillet Corn
with Bulgur

Thai Glazed Corn

Thai Glazed Corn

Total **35 min**; Serves **4**

½ **cup unsweetened coconut milk**

¼ **cup soy sauce**

2 **Tbsp. light brown sugar**

1 **Tbsp. Asian fish sauce**

1 **Tbsp. fresh lime juice, plus lime wedges for serving**

4 **ears of corn, shucked**

Chopped cilantro and finely grated Cotija cheese, for garnish

1. In a small saucepan, combine the coconut milk, soy sauce, sugar, fish sauce and lime juice. Cook over moderate heat until the glaze is syrupy, about 10 minutes.

2. Light a grill. Grill the corn over moderate heat, turning occasionally, until charred and tender, 10 to 15 minutes; brush with the glaze during the last 5 minutes. Cut each corn cob into thirds, transfer to a platter and garnish with cilantro and cheese. Serve with lime wedges.

Parmesan Corn Butter

Total **20 min**; Makes **1 cup**

1 **ear of corn, shucked**

1 **stick unsalted butter, at room temperature**

¼ **cup freshly grated Parmigiano-Reggiano cheese**

1 **tsp. finely grated lime zest**

1 **Tbsp. fresh lime juice**

Salt and pepper

In a medium cast-iron skillet, cook the corn over high heat, turning, until charred in spots, about 10 minutes. Let cool slightly. Cut the kernels off the cob and transfer to a bowl. Stir in the butter, cheese, lime zest and lime juice and season with salt and pepper.

Serve With Grilled fish, chicken or steak.

Make Ahead The corn butter can be refrigerated for up to 3 days or frozen for up to 1 month.

Cucumber Gazpacho with Shrimp

Total **15 min plus 2 hr chilling**
Serves **4**

- 4 **cucumbers–peeled, seeded and chopped**
- 1½ **cups seedless green grapes (9 oz.)**
- 1 **small garlic clove**
- ⅓ **cup extra-virgin olive oil**
- 2 **tsp. distilled white vinegar**
- **Salt**
- **Cooked shrimp and chopped roasted almonds, for garnish**

In a blender, combine the cucumbers, grapes, garlic, olive oil, vinegar and 1 cup of water; puree until smooth. Season with salt. Refrigerate until chilled, about 2 hours. Garnish with shrimp and almonds and serve.

Make Ahead The soup can be refrigerated overnight.

Wine Lively, zesty Albariño.

Cucumber and Sugar Snap Salad with Nutty Granola

Total **15 min**; Serves **6 to 8**

- ¼ **cup plus 2 Tbsp. extra-virgin olive oil**
- ¼ **cup plus 2 Tbsp. fat-free Greek yogurt**
- **Salt and pepper**
- 2 **hothouse cucumbers, cut crosswise into thirds and julienned**
- ½ **lb. sugar snap peas, thinly sliced**
- **Nutty granola, for garnish**

In a large bowl, whisk the olive oil with the yogurt and 2 tablespoons of water. Season with salt and pepper. Add the cucumbers and sugar snaps and toss to coat. Transfer the salad to plates, top with granola and serve.

Cucumber and Salami Fried Rice with Arugula

Active **20 min**; Total **40 min**; Serves **4**

- 4 **Persian or Kirby cucumbers, thinly sliced**
- **Kosher salt**
- 2 **Tbsp. canola oil**
- 3 **garlic cloves, minced**
- 3 **oz. thinly sliced salami, slivered**
- 4 **cups cooked white rice**
- 2 **scallions, thinly sliced**
- 1 **Thai or serrano chile, minced**
- 3 **oz. arugula, chopped (4 cups)**
- **Pepper**

1. In a colander set over a bowl, toss the cucumbers with 2 teaspoons of salt and let stand for 30 minutes. Rinse well and squeeze dry.

2. In a large nonstick skillet, heat the oil. Add the cucumbers, garlic and salami and cook over moderately high heat, stirring, until golden, 2 to 3 minutes. Add the rice, scallions, chile and arugula and season with salt and pepper. Stir-fry until the rice is hot, then serve.

Wine Full-bodied, melony South African Chenin Blanc.

Grilled Marinated Cucumbers and Eggplant with Basil

Total **20 min**; Serves **4**

¼ cup extra-virgin olive oil, plus more for the grill

¼ cup red wine vinegar

5 garlic cloves, minced

5 anchovy fillets, minced

Salt and pepper

4 Persian or Kirby cucumbers, quartered lengthwise

1 small eggplant, halved lengthwise and cut into wedges

Leaves from 1 small bunch of basil

Crusty bread, for serving

1. Light a grill or heat a grill pan. In a large bowl, whisk the ¼ cup of olive oil with the vinegar, garlic and anchovies; season with salt and pepper. In another large bowl, toss the cucumbers and eggplant with 3 tablespoons of the vinaigrette.

2. Oil the grate and grill the vegetables over moderate heat, turning, until the cucumbers are crisp-tender and the eggplant is tender, 3 to 5 minutes. Transfer the vegetables to the bowl with the vinaigrette and add the basil; toss to coat. Serve warm, at room temperature or cold, with bread.

BONUS RECIPE BY CHEF BOBBY FLAY

Dill Pickles

Total **20 min plus overnight pickling**; Makes **1 quart**

1½ cups distilled white vinegar

¼ cup sugar

4 tsp. kosher salt

1 tsp. mustard seeds

1 tsp. coriander seeds

¾ tsp. dill seeds

2 cups hot water

2 lbs. Kirby cucumbers, sliced ¼ inch thick

¾ cup coarsely chopped dill

3 garlic cloves, coarsely chopped

1. In a large heatproof measuring cup, combine the vinegar, sugar, salt, mustard seeds, coriander seeds and dill seeds with the hot water and stir until the sugar and salt are dissolved. Let the brine cool.

2. In a large bowl, toss the cucumbers with the dill and garlic. Pour the brine over the cucumbers and turn to coat. Place a small plate over the cucumbers to keep them submerged, then cover the bowl with plastic wrap. Refrigerate the pickles overnight, stirring once or twice. Serve cold.

Make Ahead The pickles can be refrigerated in an airtight container for up to 1 week.

Grilled Marinated
Cucumbers and
Eggplant with Basil

Eggplant

99 Pork and Eggplant Stir-Fry

99 Eggplant Noodle Salad

100 Grilled Eggplant Tortas

100 Eggplant Potato Salad

101 Baked Rigatoni with Eggplant, Tomatoes and Ricotta

Eggs

102 Mexican Eggs Baked in Tomato Sauce

103 Egg Salad with Herbs and Pickles

104 Cumin Oil–Fried Egg and Avocado Toasts

105 Sausage and Apple Frittata with Dill

Pork and Eggplant Stir-Fry

Eggplant Noodle Salad

Grilled Eggplant Torta, p. 100

Eggplant Potato Salad, p. 100

Pork and Eggplant Stir-Fry

Total **30 min**; Serves **4**

¼ **cup canola oil**

2 **baby eggplants (¾ lb.),
preferably white,
cut into ¾-inch dice**

¼ **lb. baby pattypan squash,
thinly sliced**

Salt and pepper

¾ **lb. ground pork**

5 **garlic cloves, thinly sliced**

3 **scallions, thinly sliced**

Lime wedges, for serving

In a large nonstick skillet, heat the oil. Add the eggplant and squash and season with salt and pepper. Cook over moderate heat, stirring, until the vegetables are tender, about 10 minutes. Add the pork and garlic and cook, breaking up the meat with a spoon, until the pork is browned and cooked through, about 3 minutes. Stir in the scallions and serve with lime wedges.

Wine Earthy, red-cherried Chianti Classico.

Eggplant Noodle Salad

Total **20 min**; Serves **2**

4 **oz. glass noodles**

3 **Japanese or Chinese eggplants
(1 lb.), thinly sliced crosswise**

1 **Kirby cucumber, thinly sliced**

2 **Tbsp. canola oil**

1 **tsp. finely grated peeled
fresh ginger**

½ **cup chopped basil**

¼ **cup soy sauce**

¼ **cup distilled white vinegar**

Salt and pepper

1. In a medium saucepan of boiling water, cook the noodles until al dente, about 8 minutes. Drain, rinse under cold water until cool, then drain well. Transfer to bowls.

2. In a steamer basket set over a pot of boiling water, steam the eggplant until tender, about 8 minutes. Transfer to a medium bowl. Add the cucumber, oil, ginger, basil, soy sauce and vinegar; season with salt and pepper and toss. Serve over the noodles.

Grilled Eggplant Tortas

Total **40 min**; Serves **4**

½   cup canola oil

1½ Tbsp. ground cumin

   Salt and pepper

2   medium Italian eggplants
   (2 lbs.), sliced crosswise
   ¼ inch thick

1   Hass avocado

1   Tbsp. fresh lime juice

4   soft buns, toasted

   Shredded cabbage,
   cilantro leaves and jarred
   pickled jalapeños and
   carrots, for serving

1. Heat a grill pan. In a large bowl, whisk the oil with the cumin and season with salt and pepper. Add the eggplant to the bowl and toss to coat. Working in batches, grill the eggplant slices over moderate heat, turning, until tender, about 5 minutes per batch.

2. In a small bowl, mash the avocado with the lime juice. Spread the mashed avocado on the bottom halves of the buns. Top with the eggplant, cabbage, cilantro and pickled jalapeños and carrots, close the tortas and serve.

Beer Toasty, medium-bodied brown ale.

Eggplant Potato Salad

Total **30 min**; Serves **4**

4   oz. thick-cut bacon,
   cut into lardons

2   Tbsp. extra-virgin olive oil

½   lb. baby red potatoes,
   quartered

1   small red onion, thinly sliced

2   Japanese eggplants (¾ lb.),
   quartered lengthwise and
   thinly sliced crosswise

   Salt and pepper

1   Tbsp. fresh lemon juice

2   Tbsp. chopped dill

In a large, deep skillet, cook the bacon over moderate heat, stirring, until lightly golden, about 5 minutes. Add the olive oil, potatoes, onion and eggplant and season with salt and pepper. Cover and cook over moderately low heat, stirring occasionally, until the eggplant and potatoes are tender and golden, 12 to 15 minutes. Stir in the lemon juice and dill and serve warm.

Baked Rigatoni with Eggplant, Tomatoes and Ricotta

Active **30 min**; Total **1 hr**; Serves **8**

- 4 **Tbsp. unsalted butter, plus more for greasing**
- 1 **lb. rigatoni**
- ¾ **cup extra-virgin olive oil**
- 2 **medium eggplants (2 lbs.), cut into ¾-inch dice**

  Salt and pepper
- 1 **medium onion, finely chopped**
- 4 **garlic cloves, chopped**
- 4 **beefsteak tomatoes (2 lbs.), cut into ½-inch dice**
- ⅓ **cup prepared pesto**
- 1 **cup fresh ricotta cheese**
- 6 **oz. fresh mozzarella, shredded (1½ cups)**
- ½ **cup freshly grated Parmigiano-Reggiano cheese**

1. Preheat the oven to 375°. Butter a 9-by-13-inch baking dish. In a large pot of salted boiling water, cook the rigatoni until al dente, about 8 minutes. Drain, then transfer to a large bowl. Toss the pasta with 2 tablespoons of the olive oil.

2. Meanwhile, in a large nonstick skillet, heat ¼ cup of the olive oil. Add half of the eggplant and season with salt and pepper. Cook over moderately high heat, stirring occasionally, until golden brown, about 5 minutes. Add the eggplant to the pasta. Repeat with another ¼ cup of olive oil and the remaining eggplant.

3. Add the onion, garlic and remaining 2 tablespoons of oil to the skillet. Cook over moderate heat, stirring occasionally, until the onion is lightly golden, about 5 minutes. Add the tomatoes and cook, stirring occasionally, until broken down and thickened to a sauce consistency, 7 to 8 minutes. Stir in the 4 tablespoons of butter.

4. Add the tomato sauce to the pasta and eggplant along with the pesto and ricotta; season with salt and pepper and toss well. Transfer the rigatoni to the prepared baking dish. Top with the mozzarella and Parmigiano-Reggiano and bake for about 20 minutes, until bubbling and golden on top. Let the pasta stand for 10 minutes before serving.

Wine Juicy, medium-bodied Sicilian red, like Frappato.

Mexican Eggs Baked in Tomato Sauce

Total **40 min**; Serves **4**

- 2 **Tbsp. extra-virgin olive oil**
- 3 **poblano chiles, seeded and sliced ½ inch thick**
- 3 **garlic cloves, chopped**
- 2 **cups jarred tomato sauce**
- 2 **cups halved cherry tomatoes (12 oz.)**
- 1 **tsp. dried oregano**
- 4 **large eggs**
- 1 **cup crumbled queso fresco (5 oz.)**

Chopped cilantro and sliced jalapeños, for garnish

Warm corn tortillas, for serving

Preheat the oven to 425°. In a large cast-iron skillet, heat the olive oil. Add the poblanos and garlic and cook over moderate heat, stirring, until golden, 5 minutes. Stir in the tomato sauce, tomatoes and oregano and cook over low heat until thickened, 10 minutes. Crack the eggs into the tomato sauce and top with the cheese. Bake until set, about 12 minutes. Garnish with cilantro and jalapeños and serve with corn tortillas.

Egg Salad with Herbs and Pickles

Total **20 min**; Serves 4

 8 **large eggs**

¹⁄₂ **cup Greek yogurt**

¹⁄₄ **cup chopped capers**

¹⁄₄ **cup chopped cornichons**

¹⁄₄ **cup chopped parsley**

¹⁄₄ **cup chopped tarragon**

¹⁄₄ **cup extra-virgin olive oil**

    Salt and pepper

1. In a large saucepan, cover the eggs with 1 inch of water. Bring to a full boil, then cover and remove the pan from the heat. Let stand for 10 minutes. Drain and cool the eggs under cold running water. Peel and chop the eggs.

2. In a large bowl, combine the eggs with all of the remaining ingredients, mashing with a fork, and season with salt and pepper.

Serve With Crackers or in sandwiches.

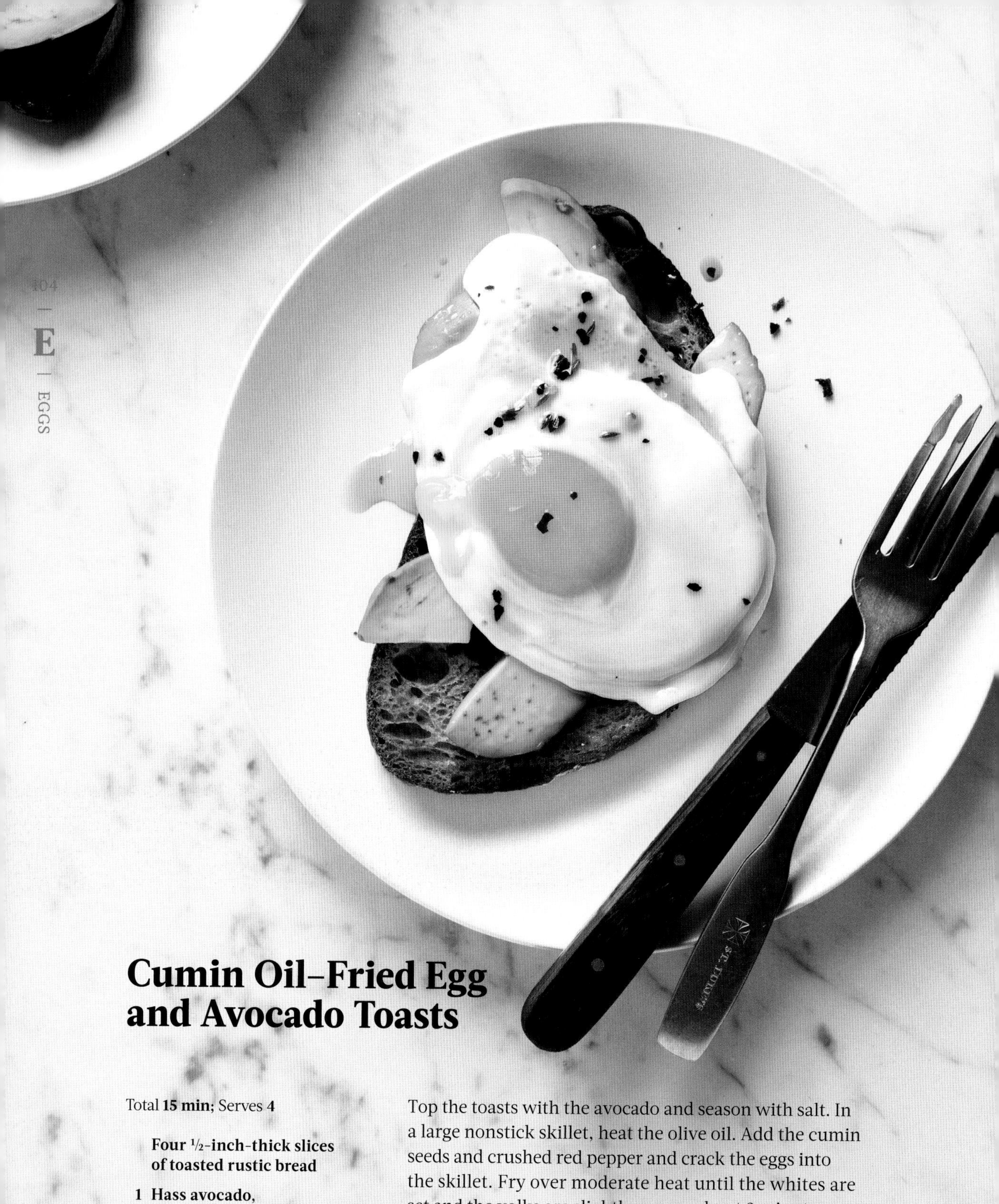

Cumin Oil–Fried Egg and Avocado Toasts

Total **15 min**; Serves **4**

Four ½-inch-thick slices of toasted rustic bread

1 **Hass avocado, sliced ½ inch thick**

Salt

3 **Tbsp. extra-virgin olive oil**

1 **tsp. cumin seeds**

1 **tsp. crushed red pepper**

4 **large eggs**

Top the toasts with the avocado and season with salt. In a large nonstick skillet, heat the olive oil. Add the cumin seeds and crushed red pepper and crack the eggs into the skillet. Fry over moderate heat until the whites are set and the yolks are slightly runny, about 3 minutes. Set the eggs on the toasts, drizzle with the cumin-pepper oil and serve.

Sausage and Apple Frittata with Dill

Active **15 min**; Total **45 min**; Serves **4**

- 1 Tbsp. extra-virgin olive oil
- ½ lb. breakfast sausage links
- 1 dozen large eggs, beaten
- ¼ cup whole milk
- 1 Granny Smith apple, peeled and cut into ¼-inch pieces
- 1 cup grated sharp cheddar cheese
- ½ cup chopped dill

  Salt and pepper

Preheat the oven to 375°. In a 9-inch ovenproof nonstick skillet, heat the oil. Add the sausage and cook over moderate heat, turning, until golden, about 5 minutes. Stir in the eggs, milk, apple, cheese and dill and season with salt and pepper. Bake until golden and set, about 30 minutes, then serve.

Wine Fresh, green apple–scented cava.

Fish Fillets & Steaks

108 **Smoky Fishwiches**

109 **Sea Bass Dill Meunière**

110 **Grilled Halibut Dip**

110 **Swordfish Spiedini**

111 **Fish Soup with Cabbage and Potatoes**

Smoky Fishwiches

Total **25 min**; Serves **4**

Canola oil, for frying

½ cup all-purpose flour

2 tsp. smoked paprika

Four 6-oz. skinless hake fillets

Salt and pepper

4 toasted kaiser rolls, mayonnaise, lettuce, tomato and pickles, for serving

In a large cast-iron skillet, heat ⅛ inch of oil. On a plate, mix the flour with the smoked paprika. Season the fish with salt and pepper, then coat in the paprika flour. Sauté the fish over moderate heat, turning, until golden outside and white throughout, 12 to 15 minutes. Spread the cut sides of the rolls with a thin layer of mayonnaise, then top with the fish, lettuce, tomato and pickles. Serve.

Wine Crisp, minerally Muscadet.

Sea Bass Dill Meunière

Total **15 min**; Serves **4**

- 2 **Tbsp. canola oil**
- **Four 6-oz. sea bass fillets**
- **Salt**
- 6 **Tbsp. unsalted butter**
- ¼ **cup drained capers**
- ¼ **cup chopped dill**
- 2 **Tbsp. fresh lemon juice**

In a large nonstick skillet, heat the oil. Season the fish with salt and cook over moderate heat, turning once, until golden outside and white throughout, about 8 minutes. Transfer to plates. Stir the butter, capers, dill and lemon juice into the skillet and cook until the butter is browned. Pour the sauce over the fish and serve.

Wine Focused, full-bodied white Burgundy.

Grilled Halibut Dip

Active **15 min**; Total **25 min**
Makes **2½ cups**

- 1 **baking potato, peeled and cut into 1-inch cubes**
- 5 **garlic cloves, peeled**
- 8 **oz. halibut fillet, about ¾ inch thick**
- 6 **Tbsp. extra-virgin olive oil**
- ½ **cup nonfat Greek yogurt**
- 2 **Tbsp. chopped chives**
  Salt and pepper
  Rye crackers or crusty bread, for serving

1. Light a grill. In a medium pot of boiling water, cook the potato and garlic until tender, about 10 minutes; drain.

2. Rub the fish all over with 1 tablespoon of the olive oil. Grill over moderate heat, turning, until white throughout, 5 to 7 minutes. Transfer to a medium bowl. Add the potato, garlic cloves, yogurt, chives and the remaining 5 tablespoons of olive oil and mash until chunky. Season with salt and pepper. Serve with rye crackers or crusty bread.

Make Ahead The dip can be refrigerated overnight.

BONUS RECIPE BY CHEF GIADA DE LAURENTIIS

Swordfish Spiedini

Total **25 min**; Serves **6**

- 2 **Tbsp. extra-virgin olive oil**
- 1 **tsp. herbes de Provence**
  Salt and pepper
- 1½ **lbs. skinless swordfish steak, cut into 1-inch cubes**
- 6 **slices of pancetta or bacon**

1. Light a grill. In a medium bowl, mix the oil with the herbes de Provence and ½ teaspoon each of salt and pepper. Add the swordfish cubes and toss to coat. Thread one-sixth of the swordfish cubes and 1 slice of pancetta onto each of 6 skewers (or soaked rosemary sprigs), wrapping the pancetta around the fish as you go.

2. Grill the spiedini over high heat, turning occasionally, until the swordfish is cooked through and lightly charred, 8 to 9 minutes. Transfer to plates and serve.

Wine Fragrant, lightly herbal Provençal rosé.

Fish Soup with Cabbage and Potatoes

Total **40 min**; Serves **4**

- **2 Tbsp. unsalted butter**
- **¼ small head of Savoy cabbage, coarsely chopped (4 cups)**
- **1 baking potato, peeled and cut into 1½-inch cubes**
- **1 qt. low-sodium chicken broth**
- **One 8-oz. bottle clam juice**
- **1 lb. cod fillet, cut into 2-inch pieces**
- **Salt and pepper**
- **Chopped scallions, for garnish**

In a large saucepan, melt the butter. Add the cabbage and potato and cook over moderate heat, stirring occasionally, until golden, 5 minutes. Stir in the broth and clam juice, bring to a simmer and cook until the potato is tender, 15 minutes. Add the fish and cook until white throughout, about 5 minutes. Season with salt and pepper, garnish with scallions and serve.

Grapes

114 **Grape and Walnut Crostini with Roquefort**

115 **Roasted Grape Cake**

116 **Fresh Grape Soda**

117 **Grape Salsa Verde**

Green Beans

118 **Bloody Mary–Pickled Green Beans**

119 **Green Bean and Scallion Pancake**

120 **Sichuan-Style Green Beans with Pork**

121 **Tempura Green Beans with Old Bay and Lemon**

Ground Beef

123 **Adobo Meat Loaves**

123 **Yorkshire Pudding Bake with Beef and Cheddar**

124 **Coconut Curried Beef Noodles**

125 **Beet and Beef Burgers**

Grape and Walnut Crostini with Roquefort

Total **20 min**; Serves **2**

- 2 Tbsp. olive oil
- 1½ cups seedless red grapes (8 oz.), halved
- 2 garlic cloves, minced
- 1 shallot, minced
- Salt and pepper
- 2 large slices of toast
- 1½ oz. Roquefort cheese, crumbled
- ¼ cup chopped walnuts

In a small saucepan, heat the olive oil. Stir in the grapes, garlic and shallot and cook over high heat, mashing, until the grapes are broken down, about 5 minutes. Season with salt and pepper and spread on the toasts. Top with the Roquefort and walnuts and serve.

Wine Fruit-forward, toasty California sparkling wine.

Roasted Grape Cake

Active **30 min**; Total **1 hr 10 min**
Makes **one 8-inch cake**

- 1 **stick unsalted butter, melted,
  plus more for greasing**

- 1 **cup self-rising flour,
  plus more for dusting**

- 3 **cups seedless red grapes (1 lb.),
  halved, plus 1 cup quartered
  grapes**

- ½ **cup honey**

- 2 **large eggs**

- 1 **tsp. pure vanilla extract**

  **Confectioners' sugar,
  for dusting**

1. Preheat the oven to 350°. Butter and flour an 8-inch-square
baking pan and line it with parchment paper. In a large
nonstick skillet, cook the 3 cups of halved grapes over high
heat, stirring, until the liquid has evaporated, 10 minutes.
Stir in the quartered grapes and spread in the prepared pan.

2. In a medium bowl, whisk the stick of melted butter with
the honey, eggs and vanilla. Whisk in the 1 cup of flour until
smooth. Pour the batter over the grapes and smooth the
surface. Bake for 30 minutes, until a toothpick inserted in the
center comes out clean. Let stand for 5 minutes, then invert
onto a rack and let cool completely. Dust with confectioners'
sugar before serving.

Make Ahead The cake can be loosely wrapped in foil and kept
at room temperature overnight.

Fresh Grape Soda

Total **30 min plus 2 hr chilling**
Makes **4 drinks**

- 3 **cups seedless red grapes (1 lb.), plus frozen red grapes for serving**
- ½ **cup sugar**
- 2 **Tbsp. fresh lime juice**
- 1 **Tbsp. minced peeled fresh ginger**
- 2 **cups chilled sparkling water**

1. In a medium saucepan, mash the 3 cups of grapes with the sugar, lime juice and ginger and bring to a boil over high heat. Cook, stirring, until syrupy, about 8 minutes. Press the grape syrup through a sieve set over a bowl and refrigerate until cold, at least 2 hours.

2. Mix the grape syrup with the sparkling water and pour into glasses. Add frozen grapes and serve.

Make Ahead The grape syrup can be refrigerated for up to 2 days.

Grape Salsa Verde

Total **20 min**; Makes **2½ cups**

- 2 **cups seedless green grapes (12 oz.), coarsely chopped**
- ¾ **cup minced yellow onion**
- ¼ **cup minced jalapeño**
- ¼ **cup minced cilantro**
- 2 **Tbsp. fresh lime juice**
- 1 **garlic clove, minced**
- **Salt and pepper**

Combine all of the ingredients in a small bowl and let stand for 10 minutes before serving.

Serve With Grilled pork or chicken.

Bloody Mary–Pickled Green Beans

Active **20 min**; Total **3 hr**
Makes **1 quart**

- 10 oz. haricots verts or other thin green beans
- 1 cup water
- ½ cup tomato juice
- ⅓ cup rice vinegar
- 2 Tbsp. prepared horseradish
- 2 Tbsp. kosher salt
- 1 tsp. black peppercorns
- 2 garlic cloves, crushed

Pack the green beans in a heatproof 1-quart glass jar. In a medium saucepan, combine all of the remaining ingredients and bring to a boil. Pour the brine over the green beans and let cool completely, then seal the jar and refrigerate for at least 2 hours before serving.

Make Ahead The pickled green beans can be refrigerated for up to 5 days.

Green Bean and Scallion Pancake

Total **30 min**; Serves **4**

- ¾ **cup all-purpose flour**
- ¾ **cup plus 2 Tbsp. chilled club soda**
- 1 **tsp. baking powder**
- ½ **tsp. kosher salt**
- ½ **tsp. toasted sesame oil**
- 2 **Tbsp. canola oil**
- 12 **oz. thin green beans, trimmed**
- 6 **scallions, cut into 3-inch lengths, plus sliced scallions for garnish**
- 1 **fresh hot red chile, thinly sliced**

  Soy sauce, for serving

1. In a medium bowl, whisk the flour with the club soda, baking powder, salt and sesame oil.

2. In a 12-inch nonstick skillet, heat the canola oil. Add the green beans and scallion pieces and stir-fry over moderately high heat until crisp-tender, about 5 minutes. Stir in the red chile and pour the batter evenly on top. Cook over moderate heat until browned on the bottom, about 5 minutes. Slide the pancake onto a plate, then invert it into the skillet and cook until browned on the second side, 3 to 5 minutes longer. Transfer to a platter and cut into wedges. Garnish with sliced scallions and serve with soy sauce.

Sichuan-Style Green Beans with Pork

Total **30 min**; Serves **4**

- **2 Tbsp. canola oil**
- **½ lb. ground pork**
- **¾ lb. green beans, thinly sliced crosswise**
- **7 to 10 dried Chinese hot red chiles, cracked**
- **2 garlic cloves, minced**
- **1½ Tbsp. soy sauce**
- **1½ Tbsp. fresh lime juice**
- **Salt and white pepper**
- **Steamed rice, for serving**

In a large skillet, heat the oil until shimmering. Add the ground pork and cook over moderately high heat, breaking it up with a fork, until nearly cooked through, about 5 minutes. Add the green beans, red chiles and garlic and stir-fry over high heat until the green beans are crisp-tender, about 7 minutes. Stir in the soy sauce and lime juice and season with salt and white pepper. Serve with steamed rice.

Wine Tropical fruit–scented, off-dry German Riesling.

Tempura Green Beans with Old Bay and Lemon

Total **30 min**; Serves **4**

Vegetable oil, for frying

1 cup all-purpose flour

2 Tbsp. cornstarch

½ tsp. baking powder

½ tsp. kosher salt

1 tsp. Old Bay seasoning, plus more for sprinkling

1 cup plus 2 Tbsp. chilled club soda

½ lb. green beans

Lemon wedges, for serving

1. In a large, deep skillet, heat ½ inch of oil until shimmering. In a large bowl, whisk the flour with the cornstarch, baking powder, salt and the 1 teaspoon of Old Bay. Gently whisk in the club soda until the batter just comes together; do not overmix.

2. Working in batches, dip the green beans in the batter, let the excess drip off and add them to the hot oil. Fry until light golden and crisp, 2 to 3 minutes. Using a slotted spoon, transfer to a paper towel–lined baking sheet to drain. Sprinkle with Old Bay and serve with lemon wedges.

Adobo Meat Loaves

Adobo Meat Loaves

Total **35 min**; Serves **4**

- 1 lb. ground beef
- ⅓ cup minced bacon
- 2 Tbsp. minced garlic
   Pepper
- ½ cup white wine vinegar
- 3 Tbsp. soy sauce
- 6 bay leaves
   Steamed white rice,
   for serving

In a medium bowl, combine the ground beef with the bacon and garlic and season with pepper. Shape the meat into four 5-inch-long oval patties and set them in a large nonstick skillet. Pour the vinegar and soy sauce around the patties and add the bay leaves. Bring to a simmer over moderate heat and cook, flipping the patties once, until the meat is cooked through and the sauce is reduced by about two-thirds, 12 minutes. Serve with rice.

Wine Smoky, meaty Washington state Syrah.

Yorkshire Pudding Bake with Beef and Cheddar

Active **15 min**; Total **40 min**
Serves **4 to 6**

- 1¼ cups whole milk
- 1 cup all-purpose flour
- 3 large eggs
- 2 Tbsp. Worcestershire sauce
- 1 tsp. salt
- ½ tsp. pepper
- 1 lb. ground beef
- 4½ oz. aged cheddar cheese, shredded (1½ cups)
- 10 sage leaves

1. Preheat the oven to 425°. In a blender, blend the milk with the flour, eggs, Worcestershire, salt and pepper.

2. In a large ovenproof skillet, cook the ground beef over high heat, stirring, until no longer pink, 3 minutes. Stir in the batter and top with the cheddar and sage leaves. Bake for about 20 minutes, until puffed and golden brown. Serve immediately.

Wine Soft, black cherry–scented California Merlot.

Coconut Curried Beef Noodles

Total **45 min**; Serves **4**

- **1 lb. ground beef**
- **¼ cup minced shallots**
- **¼ cup Thai red curry paste**
- **2 Tbsp. minced garlic**
- **2 Tbsp. minced peeled fresh ginger**
- **One 15-oz. can unsweetened coconut milk**
- **One 15-oz. can chopped tomatoes**
- **8 oz. rice noodles**
- **Sliced serrano chiles, cilantro leaves and lime wedges, for serving**

1. In a large skillet, cook the ground beef with the shallots, red curry paste, garlic and ginger over moderate heat, stirring, until browned, 8 minutes. Stir in the coconut milk and chopped tomatoes and bring to a simmer. Cook until thickened, 20 to 22 minutes.

2. Meanwhile, in a medium saucepan of boiling water, cook the noodles according to package directions. Drain and transfer to bowls.

3. Top the noodles with the meat sauce, chiles and cilantro. Serve with lime wedges.

Beer Fresh, lightly bitter Japanese lager.

Beet and Beef Burgers

Total **30 min**; Serves **4**

- 1 **lb. ground chuck**
- ½ **cup shredded cooked beets**
- ¼ **cup plain dry breadcrumbs**
- 2 **Tbsp. capers, drained and rinsed**
- 2 **Tbsp. dark lager**
- **Salt and pepper**
- 2 **Tbsp. olive oil**
- 4 **brioche buns, split and toasted**
- **Sour cream, sliced gherkins and chopped dill, for serving**

1. In a medium bowl, lightly mix the ground chuck with the beets, breadcrumbs, capers and lager and season with salt and pepper. Form into 4 round patties.

2. In a large skillet, heat the olive oil. Add the patties and cook over high heat, flipping once, 6 to 8 minutes for medium. Transfer the burgers to a plate and let rest for 5 minutes.

3. Serve the burgers on the buns, topped with sour cream, gherkins and dill.

Wine Dark-fruited, spiced Oregon Pinot Noir.

Ham

129 **Muffuletta Calzone**

129 **Spring Ham Steaks with Sweet Pea–Leek Pan Sauce**

130 **Open-Face Monte Cristos**

130 **Country Ham Flapjacks with Maple Syrup**

131 **Ham, Escarole and White Bean Stew**

Hot Peppers

132 **Crispy Baked Jalapeño Poppers**

133 **Chile-Chicken Saltimbocca**

134 **Scallops with Thai Chile Sauce**

135 **Serrano Chile and Potato Hash**

135 **Chile-Cilantro Pesto**

Muffuletta Calzone

Spring Ham Steak with
Sweet Pea–Leek Pan Sauce

Open–Face Monte Cristo, p. 130

Country Ham Flapjacks
with Maple Syrup, p. 130

Muffuletta Calzone

Total **45 min**; Serves **2 to 4**

- ½ lb. pizza dough
- 4 oz. sliced provolone cheese
- 4 oz. thinly sliced ham
- 2 oz. sliced Genoa salami
- 2 roasted bell peppers, drained
- ½ cup chopped pimiento-stuffed olives
- Extra-virgin olive oil, for brushing

Preheat the oven to 450°. On a lightly floured work surface, using a lightly floured rolling pin, roll out the dough to a 10-inch round. On one half of the dough, layer the cheese, ham, salami, bell peppers and olives. Fold the dough over the filling and crimp the edge to seal. Brush the top with olive oil and bake for about 25 minutes, until golden. Let stand for 10 minutes before cutting and serving.

Wine Vibrant, medium-bodied Italian red, such as Montepulciano.

Spring Ham Steaks with Sweet Pea–Leek Pan Sauce

Total **20 min**; Serves 4

- 4 Tbsp. unsalted butter
- Four ¼-inch-thick ham steaks (about 1 lb.)
- 1 leek, white and light green parts only, thinly sliced
- 10 oz. frozen peas, thawed
- 3 Tbsp. chopped tarragon
- Salt and pepper

In a large skillet, heat 2 tablespoons of the butter. Add the ham steaks and cook over moderate heat, turning once, until golden brown, 5 minutes. Transfer the ham to plates. Add the leek and 1½ cups of water to the skillet and cook, stirring, until the leek is softened, about 3 minutes. Stir in the peas, tarragon and the remaining 2 tablespoons of butter and season with salt and pepper. Spoon the leek-pea sauce over the ham steaks and serve.

Wine Full-bodied, pear-scented California Chardonnay.

Open-Face Monte Cristos

Total **20 min**; Serves **4**

- 4 Tbsp. unsalted butter
- ½ lb. very thinly sliced ham
- 2 large eggs
- 2 Tbsp. whole milk
- Four 1-inch-thick slices of Pullman bread
- 8 slices (½ lb.) of Gruyère cheese
- Basil leaves, for garnish

1. On a griddle, melt the butter. Cook the ham over moderate heat, turning, until golden and crispy around the edges, about 5 minutes.

2. In a shallow bowl, whisk the eggs with the milk. Dip the bread in the eggs and cook on the griddle until golden on the bottom, about 3 minutes. Flip the bread and top with the cheese and ham. Cover and cook until the cheese is melted. Garnish with basil and serve.

Wine Concentrated, full-bodied French white, such as Vouvray.

Country Ham Flapjacks with Maple Syrup

Total **20 min**; Serves **2 to 4**

- One 8½-oz. package corn muffin mix (1½ cups)
- ¾ cup buttermilk
- 1 large egg, beaten
- 6 oz. ham, chopped (1 cup)
- 1 scallion, thinly sliced
- 2 Tbsp. unsalted butter
- Pure maple syrup, for serving

In a large bowl, whisk the corn muffin mix with the buttermilk, egg, ham and scallion just until combined. In a large nonstick skillet, melt 1 tablespoon of the butter. Scoop four ¼-cup mounds of batter into the skillet and cook, turning once, until golden, about 2 minutes per side. Transfer the flapjacks to plates and repeat with the remaining butter and batter. Serve with maple syrup.

Ham, Escarole and White Bean Stew

Total **45 min**; Serves **4**

6 oz. lean slab bacon, sliced
   ¼ inch thick and cut into
   ¼-inch dice

1 Tbsp. extra-virgin olive oil,
   plus more for drizzling

1 small onion, chopped

2 garlic cloves, minced

1 Yukon Gold potato (8 oz.),
   cut into ½-inch dice

3 cups chicken or beef stock
   or low-sodium broth

6 oz. smoked ham,
   shredded (1 cup)

   One 15-oz. can cannellini
   beans, drained

½ small head of escarole,
   cut into ½-inch ribbons
   (2 packed cups)

   Freshly ground pepper

1. In a large saucepan, fry the bacon in the 1 tablespoon of olive oil over moderately high heat until browned, about 6 minutes. Spoon off all but 1 tablespoon of the fat. Add the onion and garlic and cook over moderate heat, stirring, until softened, about 5 minutes. Add the potato and cook, stirring, for 1 minute. Add the stock and boil over high heat. Reduce the heat to moderate and cook until the potato is tender, about 15 minutes.

2. Add the ham, beans and escarole to the saucepan and season with pepper. Cook over moderately high heat until the escarole is tender, about 5 minutes. Transfer to bowls, drizzle with olive oil and serve.

Crispy Baked Jalapeño Poppers

Total **35 min**; Serves **4 to 6**

- 6 oz. cream cheese, softened
- ½ cup minced pickled hot cherry peppers
- Salt
- 8 fresh jalapeños, halved lengthwise and seeded
- ⅓ cup shredded sharp cheddar cheese
- ⅓ cup panko
- 1 Tbsp. minced parsley

1. Preheat the oven to 425°. In a medium bowl, mix the cream cheese with the cherry peppers and season with salt. Fill the jalapeño halves with the cream cheese mixture and set them on a foil-lined baking sheet.

2. In a small bowl, mix the grated cheddar with the panko and parsley; sprinkle evenly over the jalapeños. Bake for 20 minutes, until the crumbs are browned, and serve.

Beer Grassy, hoppy American pale ale.

Chile-Chicken Saltimbocca

Total **25 min**; Serves **6**

- 3 **fresh long red chiles,**
  halved and seeded
- 6 **cilantro sprigs**

  Six ¹⁄₂-inch-thick chicken
  cutlets (1¹⁄₂ lbs.)

  Salt and pepper
- 4 **Tbsp. unsalted butter**

  All-purpose flour, for dredging

1. Using 2 toothpicks, secure 1 chile half and 1 cilantro sprig to one side of each chicken cutlet. Season with salt and pepper.

2. Melt 2 tablespoons of the butter in a large nonstick skillet. Lightly dredge 3 of the cutlets in flour and cook over moderately high heat, turning once, until golden outside and white throughout, about 6 minutes. Transfer to plates. Wipe out the skillet and repeat with the remaining butter and chicken. Remove the toothpicks and serve.

Wine Citrusy, herbal New Zealand Sauvignon Blanc.

Scallops with Thai Chile Sauce

Total **25 min**; Serves **4 as a starter**

- ¼ **cup plus 3 Tbsp. olive oil**
- 2 **Tbsp. minced cilantro**
- 2 **Tbsp. chopped roasted peanuts**
- 2 **Tbsp. fresh lime juice**
- 1 **Tbsp. thinly sliced red Thai chiles**
- 1 **Tbsp. minced fresh lemongrass**
- **Kosher salt**
- 12 **sea scallops**

1. In a small bowl, stir ¼ cup of the olive oil with the cilantro, peanuts, lime juice, chiles, lemongrass and ½ teaspoon of salt.

2. In a large skillet, heat the remaining 3 tablespoons of olive oil. Season the scallops with salt and cook over high heat, turning once, until golden, 3 minutes. Transfer to plates, spoon the chile sauce on top and serve.

Wine Fruity, vibrant, off-dry Riesling.

Serrano Chile and Potato Hash

Total **1 hr**; Serves **4**

- 2 Tbsp. extra-virgin olive oil
- 2 baking potatoes, peeled and cut into ½-inch dice
- 10 large serrano chiles–stemmed, quartered lengthwise and seeded
- 4 garlic cloves, thinly sliced
- 1 large white onion, thinly sliced

  Salt and pepper

  Fried eggs, cilantro leaves and sour cream, for serving

1. In a large nonstick skillet, heat the olive oil. Add the potatoes, cover and cook over moderate heat, stirring occasionally, until they begin to soften, about 10 minutes. Push the potatoes to one side of the skillet and add the chiles, garlic and onion. Cover and cook, stirring occasionally, until the onion is caramelized, about 20 minutes.

2. Stir the potatoes into the onion and chiles and season with salt and pepper. Continue to cook, stirring occasionally, until the potatoes are tender and golden, about 10 minutes longer.

3. Transfer the hash to plates and top with fried eggs and cilantro. Serve with sour cream.

BONUS RECIPE BY CHEF RICK BAYLESS

Chile-Cilantro Pesto

Total **35 min**; Makes **1 cup**

- 6 unpeeled garlic cloves
  2 to 3 serrano chiles
- 2 packed cups small parsley sprigs
- 2 packed cups small cilantro sprigs
- ½ cup extra-virgin olive oil, plus more for covering

  Salt

Heat a small cast-iron skillet. Add the garlic and chiles and cook over moderate heat, turning, until lightly charred all over, about 15 minutes. Let cool, then peel the garlic. Split the chiles lengthwise and remove most of the seeds. Coarsely chop the chiles. Transfer the garlic and chiles to a food processor or blender. Add the parsley, cilantro and the ½ cup of olive oil and puree. Season the pesto with salt and transfer to a clean jar. Pour in enough olive oil to cover the pesto by ¼ inch and refrigerate for up to 2 months.

Serve With Fish, eggs or soup.

Kale

139 Nutty Baby Kale Chips

139 Kale Rice Bowl

140 Cacio e Pepe–Style
     Braised Kale

140 Garlicky Kale-and-
     Provolone Grinders

141 Gingery Creamed Kale
     and Cabbage

Nutty Baby Kale Chips

Kale Rice Bowl

Cacio e Pepe–Style Braised Kale, p. 140

Garlicky Kale-
and-Provolone
Grinders, p. 140

Nutty Baby Kale Chips

Active **15 min**; Total **35 min plus cooling**; Makes **4 cups**

½ cup raw almond butter

¼ cup canola oil

Salt

4 cups baby kale leaves

Preheat the oven to 325°. Set 2 racks on 2 large baking sheets. In a large bowl, whisk the almond butter with the oil and season with salt. Add the kale leaves and massage to coat. Arrange the kale on the racks in single layers and bake for about 20 minutes, rotating the baking sheets, until the leaves are golden and almost crisp. Let cool completely before serving; the chips will crisp up as they cool.

Kale Rice Bowl

Total **30 min**; Serves **4**

2 Tbsp. canola oil

5 garlic cloves, thinly sliced

2 Tbsp. chopped peeled fresh ginger

¾ lb. ground pork

1 lb. red kale (2 bunches), stemmed, leaves torn into large pieces (16 cups)

1 Tbsp. Asian fish sauce

1 cup mixed chopped basil and cilantro

Salt and pepper

Steamed rice and Sriracha, for serving

In a large nonstick skillet, heat the canola oil. Add the garlic, ginger and pork and cook over moderate heat, stirring, until the pork is just cooked through, about 3 minutes. In batches, add the kale and stir-fry until tender, about 5 minutes. Stir in the fish sauce and herbs and season with salt and pepper. Serve with rice and Sriracha.

Wine Full-bodied, apple- and pear-scented Oregon Pinot Gris.

Cacio e Pepe–Style Braised Kale

Active **10 min**; Total **25 min**; Serves **4**

2 Tbsp. unsalted butter

2 Tbsp. extra-virgin olive oil

1 lb. Tuscan kale (2 bunches), stemmed, leaves torn into large pieces (16 cups)

2 cups low-sodium chicken broth

Salt

Pinch of crushed red pepper

Cracked black pepper

⅓ cup freshly grated Parmigiano-Reggiano cheese

In a large pot, melt the butter in the olive oil. Add the kale in batches and cook over moderate heat, stirring, until wilted, about 3 minutes. Add the broth and bring to a simmer. Cover and cook until the kale is tender and almost all of the broth is absorbed, about 10 minutes. Season with salt. Transfer the kale to a platter and top with the crushed red pepper, lots of black pepper and the cheese.

Garlicky Kale-and-Provolone Grinders

Active **20 min**; Total **40 min**; Serves **4**

2 Tbsp. extra-virgin olive oil

7 oil-packed anchovy fillets

5 garlic cloves, minced

1 lb. green kale (2 bunches), stemmed, leaves torn into large pieces (about 18 cups)

½ lb. thinly sliced provolone cheese

One 12-inch ciabatta loaf, halved horizontally

Thinly sliced radishes, chopped green olives and mayonnaise, for serving

1. In a large nonstick skillet, heat the olive oil. Add the anchovies and garlic, then add the kale in batches and cook over moderate heat, stirring, until the kale is wilted, about 3 minutes. Add 1 cup of water, cover and cook until tender, 15 minutes. Top the kale with the cheese in an even layer, cover and cook until the cheese melts, 2 minutes.

2. Using a large slotted spoon, transfer the kale and cheese to the bottom half of the ciabatta, then top with radishes and olives. Spread the top half of the ciabatta with mayonnaise and close the sandwich. Cut into 4 pieces and serve.

Gingery Creamed Kale and Cabbage

Active **30 min**; Total **1 hr**
Serves **12**

Salt

3 lbs. kale, tough stems
   discarded

¼ cup plus 2 Tbsp. vegetable oil

1 large white onion,
   coarsely chopped

1 lb. green cabbage,
   coarsely shredded

1½ Tbsp. finely grated peeled
   fresh ginger

½ tsp. turmeric

2 cups heavy cream

1 cup buttermilk

1. Bring a large pot of water to a boil and salt the water. Add the kale leaves and cook until tender, about 6 minutes. Drain and let cool, then coarsely chop.

2. In the same pot, heat the oil. Add the onion and cook over moderate heat until softened, about 7 minutes. Add the cabbage, ginger and turmeric and season with salt. Cook over moderate heat, stirring occasionally, until the cabbage is wilted, about 5 minutes. Add the cream, cover and simmer over moderately low heat, stirring occasionally, until the cream is thickened, about 8 minutes. Stir in the kale, season with salt and cook for 3 minutes, stirring a few times. Remove from the heat and stir in the buttermilk. Bring to a simmer and serve.

Make Ahead The kale can be refrigerated overnight. Reheat gently and stir in the buttermilk shortly before serving.

Lamb

144 **Coconut Lamb Curry with Sweet Potatoes**

145 **Simplest Lamb Bolognese with Pappardelle**

146 **Grilled Lamb Loin Chops with Pomegranate Relish**

147 **Spiced Lamb Sliders with Harissa Mayonnaise and Cucumber**

Lentils

148 **Warm Lentil and Carrot Salad with Feta Dressing**

148 **Yellow Lentil Dal with Tofu**

150 **Fried Spiced Red Lentils**

150 **Lentil and Chicken Cassoulet**

Coconut Lamb Curry with Sweet Potatoes

Active **30 min**; Total **1 hr 30 min**
Serves **4**

1 Tbsp. canola oil

2¼ lbs. trimmed lamb shoulder, cut into 1-inch cubes

Salt and pepper

2 Tbsp. minced garlic

2 Tbsp. minced peeled fresh ginger

1 Tbsp. Madras curry powder

1½ cups chicken stock or low-sodium broth

One 14-oz. can unsweetened coconut milk

2 medium sweet potatoes, peeled and cut into 1-inch dice

Chopped cilantro and toasted unsweetened coconut flakes, for garnish

Lime wedges and steamed rice, for serving

1. In a large pot, heat the oil until shimmering. Season the lamb with salt and pepper, add it to the pot and cook over moderately high heat, turning occasionally, until browned, about 8 minutes. Add the garlic, ginger and curry powder and cook until fragrant, about 30 seconds. Stir in the stock and coconut milk and bring to a boil. Cover and simmer over moderately low heat until the lamb is tender, about 45 minutes.

2. Add the sweet potatoes to the curry and simmer until tender, about 15 minutes. Spoon into bowls and garnish with chopped cilantro and toasted coconut. Serve with lime wedges and steamed rice.

Make Ahead The curry can be refrigerated overnight. Reheat gently before serving.

Wine Fruit-forward, full-bodied Rhône white.

Simplest Lamb Bolognese with Pappardelle

Active **30 min**; Total **1 hr 15 min**
Serves **4**

- 2 Tbsp. olive oil
- 1½ lbs. ground lamb
- 1 red onion, finely chopped
- 3 garlic cloves, minced
- 2 tsp. fennel seeds
- Salt and pepper
- One 15-oz. can crushed tomatoes
- 1½ cups chicken stock or low-sodium broth
- ½ lb. pappardelle
- Freshly grated Pecorino Romano cheese, for serving

1. In a large saucepan, heat the olive oil. Add the lamb, onion, garlic, fennel seeds and a generous pinch each of salt and pepper. Cook over moderately high heat, stirring occasionally, until the lamb is cooked through, 8 to 10 minutes. Add the tomatoes and stock and bring to a boil. Cover partially and simmer over moderately low heat, stirring occasionally, until the sauce is thick, about 40 minutes. Season the Bolognese with salt and pepper.

2. In a large pot of salted boiling water, cook the pasta until al dente. Drain well, reserving ½ cup of the cooking water. Add the pasta and reserved cooking water to the sauce and cook over moderately low heat, tossing, until coated. Transfer the pasta to bowls and serve with grated cheese.

Make Ahead The Bolognese can be refrigerated for up to 5 days. Reheat gently before serving.

Wine Vibrant, medium-bodied Italian red, like Barbera.

Grilled Lamb Loin Chops
with Pomegranate Relish

Total **30 min**; Serves **4 to 6**

Eight 7- to 8-oz. lamb loin chops, cut 2 inches thick

Salt and pepper

1½ **cups pomegranate seeds (from 2 pomegranates)**

1 **lightly packed cup mint, chopped, plus whole leaves for garnish**

1 **shallot, minced**

3 **Tbsp. extra-virgin olive oil**

2 **Tbsp. sherry vinegar**

1. Light a grill or heat a cast-iron grill pan. Season the lamb chops with salt and pepper and grill over moderate heat, turning occasionally, until lightly charred all over and an instant-read thermometer inserted in the thickest part of the chops registers 130°, about 15 minutes. Transfer to a platter and let rest for 5 minutes.

2. In a medium bowl, mix the pomegranate seeds with the chopped mint, shallot, olive oil and vinegar; season with salt and pepper. Serve the relish with the lamb chops, garnished with mint leaves.

Wine Dark-berried New Zealand Pinot Noir.

Spiced Lamb Sliders with Harissa Mayonnaise and Cucumber

Total **30 min**; Makes **12 sliders**

- ½ cup mayonnaise
- 2 Tbsp. harissa
- 1 lb. ground lamb
- 1 tsp. ground coriander
- 1 tsp. ground cumin
- 1 tsp. paprika

  Kosher salt and pepper
- 12 brioche dinner rolls, split and toasted

  Thinly sliced English cucumber, for serving

1. Light a grill or heat a grill pan. In a small bowl, whisk the mayonnaise with the harissa.

2. In a large bowl, mix the lamb with the coriander, cumin, paprika and 1 teaspoon each of salt and pepper. Form the mixture into twelve ½-inch-thick patties and grill over high heat, turning once, until lightly charred outside and medium within, about 4 minutes. Set the patties on the rolls, top with the harissa mayonnaise and cucumber and serve.

Wine Lively, red berry–scented Côtes du Rhône.

Warm Lentil and Carrot Salad with Feta Dressing

Active **15 min**; Total **45 min**
Serves **4 to 6**

- 1 lb. carrots–peeled, halved lengthwise and cut into 3-inch pieces
- 7 Tbsp. extra-virgin olive oil
- ¾ cup French green (Le Puy) lentils
- 1 cup chopped cucumber
- ¼ cup chopped dill
- Salt and pepper
- ½ cup crumbled feta cheese

1. Preheat the oven to 450°. On a baking sheet, toss the carrots with 2 tablespoons of the olive oil and roast until tender, about 30 minutes. Scrape into a large serving bowl.

2. Meanwhile, in a small saucepan of boiling water, cook the lentils until al dente, about 15 minutes. Drain well.

3. Add the lentils to the carrots along with the cucumber, dill and 2 tablespoons of the oil; season with salt and pepper.

4. In a blender, puree the feta with 2 tablespoons of water and the remaining 3 tablespoons of oil until smooth. Season with salt. Spoon the dressing over the lentil salad and serve.

Wine Crisp, lightly herbal Sauvignon Blanc.

Yellow Lentil Dal with Tofu

Active **20 min**; Total **50 min**
Serves **4 to 6**

- 2 Tbsp. canola oil
- ½ red onion, minced (⅓ cup)
- ½ tomato, minced (⅓ cup)
- 2 Tbsp. minced garlic
- 2 Tbsp. minced peeled fresh ginger
- 1 tsp. coriander seeds
- 1 tsp. cumin seeds
- 1 cup yellow lentils
- 12 oz. soft tofu, cubed
- Chopped cilantro, for garnish

In a large saucepan, heat the oil. Add the onion, tomato, garlic, ginger, coriander and cumin and cook over moderate heat, stirring, until the aromatics are golden, about 5 minutes. Stir in the lentils and 6 cups of water and bring to a boil. Cover and simmer gently over moderately low heat until the lentils are tender and the dal is thickened, 30 minutes. Fold in the tofu and cook until warmed through. Garnish with cilantro and serve.

Wine Creamy, yellow apple–inflected California Chardonnay.

Warm Lentil and Carrot Salad
with Feta Dressing

Fried Spiced Red Lentils

Active **10 min**; Total **1 hr 10 min**
Makes **1½ cups**

- 2 **cups red lentils, soaked for 1 hour and drained**

  Canola oil, for frying
- ¼ **tsp. smoked paprika**

  Salt and pepper

Pat the lentils dry with paper towels. In a large cast-iron skillet, heat ¼ inch of oil until shimmering. Fry the lentils in batches, stirring, until yellow and crisp, about 2 minutes. Transfer to a paper towel–lined plate to drain. In a small bowl, toss the fried lentils with the paprika, season with salt and pepper and serve.

Lentil and Chicken Cassoulet

Active **15 min**; Total **1 hr**; Serves **4**

- 2 **Tbsp. olive oil**
- 6 **chicken legs (3 lbs.)**
- 8 **garlic cloves, crushed**
- 1 **lb. sausages, such as Italian or merguez**
- 3 **cups low-sodium chicken broth**
- 1 **tarragon sprig, plus chopped tarragon for garnish**
- 2 **cups beluga lentils**

  Salt and pepper

In a large enameled cast-iron casserole, heat the oil. Add the chicken and garlic and cook over moderate heat, turning, until browned, about 8 minutes. Add the sausages, broth and tarragon sprig and bring to a boil. Simmer for 15 minutes. Stir in the lentils, cover and cook over moderate heat until tender, about 30 minutes. Remove the tarragon sprig. Season the cassoulet with salt and pepper, garnish with chopped tarragon and serve.

Wine Earthy, focused red Burgundy.

Fried Spiced
Red Lentils

Mushrooms

155 **Mushroom Carpaccio with Chive Oil**

155 **Garlicky Mushroom Pasta with Parsley**

156 **Warm Mushroom–Barley Salad**

157 **Mushroom Poutine**

Mushroom Carpaccio
with Chive Oil

Mushroom Carpaccio with Chive Oil

Total **25 min**; Serves **4**

- **1 cup chopped chives**
- **½ cup extra-virgin olive oil**
- **Salt**
- **8 oz. very fresh white mushrooms, very thinly sliced on a mandoline**
- **1 Tbsp. fresh lemon juice**
- **Chopped roasted almonds and freshly shaved Parmigiano-Reggiano cheese, for garnish**

In a blender, combine the chives and oil and puree until smooth. Strain the chive oil through a sieve and season with salt. Spread the mushrooms on a platter. Drizzle with the lemon juice and chive oil. Garnish with chopped almonds and shaved cheese and serve.

Garlicky Mushroom Pasta with Parsley

Total **30 min**; Serves **4**

- **12 oz. orecchiette**
- **¼ cup extra-virgin olive oil**
- **1 lb. small cremini mushrooms, halved if large**
- **5 garlic cloves, finely chopped**
- **4 Tbsp. unsalted butter**
- **¼ cup chopped parsley**
- **Salt and pepper**
- **Lemon wedges, for serving**

1. In a large pot of salted boiling water, cook the pasta until al dente. Drain, reserving ½ cup of the cooking water.

2. Meanwhile, in a large skillet, heat the olive oil. Add the mushrooms and garlic and cook over moderate heat, stirring occasionally, until golden and tender, about 8 minutes.

3. Stir the pasta, reserved cooking water and the butter and parsley into the mushrooms and cook, tossing, until saucy, about 2 minutes; season with salt and pepper. Serve with lemon wedges.

Wine Minerally, lemon-zesty Sancerre.

Warm Mushroom–Barley Salad

Total **50 min**; Serves 4

- 1 **cup barley**
- ¼ **cup extra-virgin olive oil**
- 12 **oz. shiitake mushrooms, stemmed and thinly sliced**
- 5 **shallots, thinly sliced (2 cups)**
- 2 **Tbsp. fresh lemon juice**
- **Salt and pepper**
- **Sliced scallions, for garnish**

1. In a large saucepan of boiling water, cook the barley until tender, about 30 minutes. Drain.

2. Meanwhile, in a large skillet, heat the olive oil. Add the mushrooms and shallots and cook over moderate heat, stirring, until golden and tender, 5 to 7 minutes. Stir in the lemon juice and barley and season with salt and pepper. Transfer to a serving dish and garnish with scallions.

Mushroom Poutine

Active **15 min**; Total **1 hr**; Serves **4**

- 1 **lb. maitake mushrooms, torn into large pieces**
- 7 **oz. store-bought frozen sweet potato fries, such as Alexia**
- ¼ **cup extra-virgin olive oil**
- 2 **Tbsp. unsalted butter**
- 2 **Tbsp. all-purpose flour**
- ¾ **cup whole milk**
- **Salt and pepper**
- 3½ **oz. Fontina cheese, shredded (1 cup)**

1. Preheat the oven to 425°. In a 3-quart baking dish, toss the mushrooms with the fries and olive oil. Bake until the fries are crispy, about 45 minutes. Remove from the oven and turn on the broiler.

2. Meanwhile, in a small saucepan, melt the butter. Add the flour and cook, whisking, until golden, 5 minutes. Whisk in the milk and cook until thickened, about 3 minutes. Season with salt and pepper. Spoon the gravy over the mushrooms and fries and top with the cheese. Broil 6 inches from the heat until golden, about 5 minutes.

Beer Nutty, malty brown ale.

Oranges

160 **Honey-Orange Chicken**

160 **Roasted Orange Marmalade**

162 **Orange Caramel Sauce**

163 **Orange-Almond Parfaits**

Honey-Orange Chicken

Total **1 hr**; Serves 4

- 8 boneless, skin-on chicken thighs
- 1 cup fresh orange juice
- 1 Tbsp. minced rosemary
- 1 Tbsp. minced garlic

  Salt and pepper
- 2 Tbsp. honey
- 2 Tbsp. sesame seeds
- 1 tsp. finely grated orange zest
- 1 fresh long red chile, thinly sliced into rings

1. In a large bowl, toss the chicken with the orange juice, rosemary and garlic and marinate at room temperature for 30 minutes.

2. Light a grill. Remove the chicken from the marinade and season with salt and pepper. Starting with the skin side down, grill the chicken over moderately high heat, turning once, until white throughout, 18 to 20 minutes. Transfer to a platter and drizzle with the honey. Sprinkle the chicken with the sesame seeds, orange zest and chile before serving.

Wine Fruit-forward, medium-bodied white, like California Sauvignon Blanc.

Roasted Orange Marmalade

Active **20 min**; Total **1 hr plus cooling**; Makes **2⅔ cups**

- 2 navel oranges–washed well, ends trimmed, halved crosswise
- 2 cups sugar
- ½ cup fresh orange juice
- 2 Tbsp. fresh lemon juice
- ½ tsp. kosher salt
- ½ cup pomegranate seeds

1. Preheat the oven to 425°. Place the orange halves cut side down on a foil-lined baking sheet and roast for 40 minutes, until caramelized. Let cool for 5 minutes.

2. Transfer the oranges to a food processor and pulse until finely chopped. Scrape into a medium saucepan and stir in the sugar, orange juice, lemon juice and salt. Bring to a boil over high heat and cook, stirring, until thickened, about 6 minutes. Let the marmalade cool completely, then stir in the pomegranate seeds and serve.

Make Ahead The marmalade can be refrigerated for up to 1 week.

Honey-Orange Chicken

Orange Caramel Sauce

Total **10 min plus cooling**
Makes **1 cup**

1 cup sugar

½ cup fresh orange juice

Vanilla ice cream and
flaky sea salt, for serving

1. In a small skillet, combine the sugar with ¼ cup of water and cook over high heat, swirling the pan often, until an amber caramel forms, about 6 minutes. Remove the skillet from the heat and carefully pour in the orange juice; swirl to combine. Let cool.

2. To serve, spoon the caramel sauce over vanilla ice cream and sprinkle with a pinch of flaky salt.

Make Ahead The sauce can be refrigerated for up to 1 week.

Orange-Almond Parfaits

Total **25 min**; Serves **4**

  4 navel oranges

 24 medium amaretti cookies
     (about 5 oz.), crushed

  1 cup heavy cream, whipped

 ½ cup chopped toasted almonds

Using a sharp knife, peel the oranges, removing all of the bitter white pith. Working over a bowl, cut the oranges in between the membranes and release the sections into the bowl. Layer half of the orange sections in 4 glasses and top with half of the crushed amaretti cookies, whipped cream and almonds. Repeat the layering once more and serve.

Pasta

166   Fettuccine with Shrimp

167   Cacio e Pepe Pasta Pie

168   Penne with Chicken
and Pickled Peppers

169   Orecchiette with Sausage,
Chickpeas and Mint

Peppers

171   Herb-Marinated Peppers
and Tuna

171   Mixed Bell Pepper Pasta

172   Spicy Pickled Peppers

172   Bulgogi-Style Pepper Steak
Sandwiches

173   Chicken and Pepper
Cacciatore

Pork

174   Spicy Fideos with Pork

175   Fennel-Rubbed Pork
Tenderloin with Fingerling
Potatoes and Lemon

177   Blackberry-Glazed Pork
Chops with Broccolini

177   Vietnamese Pork Burgers

Potatoes

179   Warm Potato and
Green Bean Salad

179   Crispy Buffalo-Style
Potatoes

180   Accordion Potatoes

180   Potato-Apple-Dill Pancakes

181   Boiled Potatoes with
Sage Butter

181   Tortilla Española

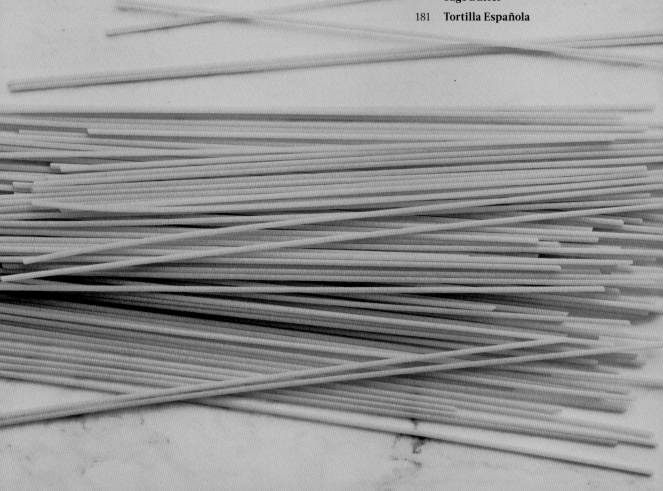

Fettuccine with Shrimp

Total **30 min**; Serves **4**

12 oz. fettuccine

4 Tbsp. unsalted butter

8 scallions, thinly sliced

3 garlic cloves, thinly sliced

¾ cup dry white wine

⅔ cup mascarpone cheese

12 oz. cooked shrimp

6 oz. curly spinach leaves

Salt and pepper

1. In a large pot of salted boiling water, cook the pasta until al dente. Drain.

2. Wipe out the pot; melt the butter in it. Add the scallions and garlic and cook over moderately high heat until softened, 2 minutes. Add the wine and simmer until reduced by half, about 3 minutes. Stir in the mascarpone. Add the pasta and shrimp and cook, tossing, until the pasta is coated, 3 minutes. Stir in the spinach and season with salt and pepper. Serve hot.

Wine Lemon-zesty Italian white, like Vermentino.

Cacio e Pepe Pasta Pie

Active **30 min**; Total **1 hr 30 min**
Serves **8**

- **1 lb.** spaghetti
- **1½ cups** milk
- **¾ cup** freshly grated Parmigiano-Reggiano cheese
- **3 large** eggs, lightly beaten
- **2½ tsp.** ground black pepper
- **2 tsp.** kosher salt
- **6 oz.** Fontina cheese, shredded (2 cups)
- **6 oz.** sharp white cheddar cheese, shredded (2 cups)
- Butter, for greasing

1. Preheat the oven to 425°. In a pot of salted boiling water, cook the spaghetti until al dente. Drain well.

2. In a large bowl, mix the pasta, milk, Parmigiano, eggs, pepper, salt and 1½ cups each of the Fontina and cheddar. Scrape into a buttered 9-inch springform pan, then sprinkle the remaining ½ cup each of Fontina and cheddar on top. Bake for 35 to 40 minutes, until the cheese is melted and bubbling.

3. Turn on the broiler. Broil the pie 8 inches from the heat for 2 to 3 minutes, until browned on top. Transfer to a rack and let cool for 15 minutes. Remove the ring, cut the pie into wedges and serve.

Wine Silky, concentrated northern Italian red.

Penne with Chicken and Pickled Peppers

Total **30 min**; Serves **4**

12 oz. penne rigate

1½ **cups shredded cooked chicken**

1½ **cups sliced mixed pickled peppers, drained**

½ **cup extra-virgin olive oil**

Salt

1 **cup basil leaves**

1. In a pot of salted boiling water, cook the penne until al dente. Drain, reserving ½ cup of the cooking water.

2. Wipe out the pot; add the chicken, peppers and oil. Cook over moderate heat, stirring occasionally, until hot, about 6 minutes. Add the penne and cooking water and cook, tossing, until hot, about 3 minutes. Season with salt, stir in the basil and serve.

Wine Fresh, juicy pear-scented Italian white, like Arneis.

Orecchiette with Sausage, Chickpeas and Mint

Total **30 min**; Serves **6**

- 1 lb. orecchiette
- ⅓ cup extra-virgin olive oil
- ¾ lb. loose sweet Italian sausage
- 1 large red onion, thinly sliced
- One 15-oz. can chickpeas, rinsed
- 1 cup small mint leaves
- 2 Tbsp. fresh lemon juice
- Salt and pepper
- Yogurt, for serving

1. In a pot of salted boiling water, cook the orecchiette until al dente. Drain, reserving ¾ cup of the cooking water.

2. Wipe out the pot and heat the olive oil in it. Add the sausage and cook over moderate heat, breaking up the meat with a wooden spoon, until browned and nearly cooked through, about 7 minutes. Add the onion and cook, stirring occasionally, until softened, about 3 minutes. Add the chickpeas, orecchiette and reserved cooking water and toss over moderate heat until the pasta is hot and coated in a light sauce, about 2 minutes. Stir in the mint and lemon juice and season with salt and pepper. Spoon the pasta into bowls and serve with yogurt.

Wine Vibrant, spice-inflected Barbera d'Alba.

Herb-Marinated Peppers and Tuna

Mixed Bell Pepper Pasta

Spicy Pickled Peppers, p. 172

Bulgogi-Style Pepper
Steak Sandwiches, p. 172

Herb-Marinated Peppers and Tuna

Active **15 min**; Total **40 min**
Serves **6 to 8**

- 2 **cups extra-virgin olive oil**
- 1 **head of garlic, cloves peeled and crushed**
- 4 **poblano peppers (1 lb.), sliced lengthwise into ½-inch-wide strips**
- ⅓ **cup drained capers**

  16 oz. **good-quality tuna in olive oil, drained**
- ½ **cup basil leaves**

  Lemon wedges and crusty bread, for serving

Preheat the oven to 450°. In a baking dish, combine the olive oil, garlic, poblanos and capers. Roast for 20 minutes, until the poblanos are tender. Let cool until warm, then stir in the tuna and basil. Serve with lemon wedges and bread.

Wine Herb-scented, citrusy New Zealand Sauvignon Blanc.

Mixed Bell Pepper Pasta

Total **30 min**; Serves **4 to 6**

- 2 **Tbsp. extra-virgin olive oil, plus more for drizzling**
- 1 **small onion, finely chopped**
- 5 **garlic cloves, finely chopped**
- 1½ **lbs. mixed bell peppers, finely chopped**

  Salt and black pepper
- 1 **lb. spaghetti**
- 1 **cup cherry tomatoes, halved**
- ¼ **cup chopped flat-leaf parsley**

1. In a large skillet, heat the 2 tablespoons of olive oil. Add the onion, garlic and bell peppers, season with salt and black pepper and cook over moderate heat, stirring occasionally, until the peppers are tender, about 10 minutes.

2. Meanwhile, in a pot of salted boiling water, cook the pasta until al dente. Drain, reserving 1 cup of the cooking water.

3. Add the spaghetti, reserved cooking water, tomatoes and parsley to the skillet and toss over moderate heat for 1 minute. Serve, drizzled with olive oil.

Wine Bright, fruit-forward Italian rosé.

Spicy Pickled Peppers

Total **15 min plus 2 hr cooling**
Makes **1 quart**

12 oz. mixed peppers, such as bell, jalapeño and serrano, sliced (with seeds)

1½ cups distilled white vinegar

1 Tbsp. kosher salt

2 tsp. caraway seeds

1 tsp. sugar

Put the peppers in a 1-quart mason jar. In a medium saucepan, combine ½ cup of water with the vinegar, salt, caraway seeds and sugar. Stir over low heat until the sugar and salt dissolve. Pour the brine over the peppers and let stand until cool, about 2 hours.

Serve With Grilled sausages or steak.

Make Ahead The pickled peppers can be refrigerated for up to 1 week.

Bulgogi-Style Pepper Steak Sandwiches

Total **30 min**; Serves **4**

¼ cup canola oil, plus more for the grill

½ cup low-sodium soy sauce

7 garlic cloves, minced

1 Tbsp. minced peeled fresh ginger

2 green bell peppers, thinly sliced

2 bunches of scallions, halved crosswise

1 lb. rib eye steak, thinly sliced (see Note)

Toasted soft hoagie buns, mayonnaise and sliced pickles, for serving

Light a grill and oil the grate. In a large bowl, whisk the ¼ cup of oil with the soy sauce, garlic and ginger. Add the peppers, scallions and meat and toss to coat. Grill over moderately high heat, turning, 1 to 2 minutes for the meat, 3 minutes for the scallions and about 8 minutes for the peppers. Assemble the sandwiches on buns with mayo and pickles.

Note Look for thinly sliced steak at Asian markets or have your butcher slice it.

Beer Hop-forward pale ale.

Chicken and Pepper Cacciatore

Active **30 min**; Total **1 hr**
Serves **4**

- 2 Tbsp. extra-virgin olive oil
- 8 boneless chicken thighs (3 lbs.)
  Salt and pepper
- 1 medium onion, thinly sliced
- 1 red bell pepper, thinly sliced
- 2 pickled hot peppers, thinly sliced
- 3 garlic cloves, thinly sliced
- ½ cup dry red wine
- 1½ cups chicken stock or low-sodium broth
- 1 lb. ripe plum tomatoes, coarsely chopped
- 2 Tbsp. chopped flat-leaf parsley

1. In a large, deep skillet, heat the olive oil. Season the chicken thighs with salt and pepper and add to the skillet, skin side down. Cook over moderately high heat, turning once, until lightly browned and crisp, about 8 minutes. Transfer to a plate.

2. Add the onion, bell pepper, pickled peppers and garlic to the skillet and cook over low heat, stirring occasionally, until softened, about 10 minutes. Pour in the wine and simmer, stirring occasionally, until nearly evaporated, about 5 minutes.

3. Add the chicken stock and tomatoes to the skillet and season lightly with salt and pepper. Return the chicken to the pan, nestling it in the vegetables skin side up, and bring to a simmer. Cover partially and cook over moderate heat for 30 minutes, until the chicken is tender and the sauce is reduced by half. Sprinkle with the parsley and serve.

Wine Earthy, cherry-inflected Italian red, like Sangiovese.

Spicy Fideos with Pork

Total **30 min**; Serves **4 to 6**

- 6 Tbsp. unsalted butter
- 12 oz. angel hair pasta, broken
- 12 oz. ground pork
- 2 chipotles in adobo, minced
- 1½ tsp. crushed cumin seeds
-   One 15-oz. can tomato puree
- 3½ cups chicken stock or low-sodium broth
-   Salt
-   Cilantro leaves, sliced radishes and lime wedges, for serving

1. In a large saucepan, melt the butter. Add the broken pasta and cook, stirring, until browned all over, 5 to 7 minutes. Transfer the toasted pasta to a medium bowl.

2. Add the pork, chipotles and cumin seeds to the saucepan and cook over moderate heat, stirring, until the meat is browned, about 5 minutes. Stir in the tomato puree and stock and bring to a boil. Stir in the toasted pasta and simmer over moderately high heat, stirring, until the pasta is al dente and coated in a thick sauce, 5 to 7 minutes. Season with salt. Spoon the fideos into shallow bowls and serve right away, with cilantro, sliced radishes and lime wedges.

Wine Robustly fruity Spanish rosé.

Fennel-Rubbed Pork Tenderloin with Fingerling Potatoes and Lemon

Total **40 min**; Serves **4**

1½ **lbs. fingerling potatoes, sliced ¼ inch thick**

1 **lemon, thinly sliced crosswise**

4 **thyme sprigs**

3 **Tbsp. extra-virgin olive oil, plus more for brushing**

Salt and pepper

One 1¼-lb. pork tenderloin

1 **Tbsp. crushed fennel seeds**

1. Preheat the oven to 450°. On a large rimmed baking sheet, toss the potatoes with the lemon, thyme and 3 tablespoons of olive oil. Season generously with salt and pepper.

2. Brush the pork with olive oil. Rub the fennel all over the pork and season with salt and pepper. Set the pork on the potatoes and roast for about 25 minutes, until an instant-read thermometer inserted in the thickest part of the meat registers 135°. Transfer the pork to a carving board and let rest for 5 minutes, then slice and serve with the potatoes and lemon.

Wine Fragrant, dry Provençal rosé.

Blackberry-Glazed
Pork Chops
with Broccolini

Blackberry-Glazed Pork Chops with Broccolini

Total **45 min**; Serves **4**

- ½ cup blackberry preserves
- 2 Tbsp. barbecue sauce
- 1 Tbsp. Dijon mustard
-   Four 12-oz. bone-in pork loin chops (with the tenderloin), cut 1½ inches thick
-   Salt and pepper
- 1 lb. Broccolini
- 2 Tbsp. extra-virgin olive oil

1. Light a grill or heat a grill pan. In a small bowl, whisk the preserves with the barbecue sauce and mustard. Season the pork chops with salt and pepper and grill over moderate heat, turning occasionally, until lightly charred and nearly cooked through, about 15 minutes. Brush the chops with the blackberry glaze and cook, turning and glazing frequently, until an instant-read thermometer inserted near the bone registers 140°, about 5 minutes longer. Transfer the chops to a carving board to rest for 5 minutes.

2. Meanwhile, in a large bowl, toss the Broccolini with the olive oil and season with salt and pepper. Grill over moderately high heat, turning, until lightly charred and crisp-tender, 3 to 5 minutes.

3. Serve the pork chops with the Broccolini, passing any remaining glaze at the table.

Make Ahead The blackberry glaze can be refrigerated for up to 1 week.

Wine Bold, blackberry-inflected California Cabernet.

Vietnamese Pork Burgers

Total **30 min**; Serves **4**

- 1½ lbs. ground pork
-   Salt
- ¾ cup mayonnaise
- 1 Tbsp. Sriracha
- ¾ tsp. toasted sesame oil
- 4 brioche burger buns, split and toasted
-   Shredded carrot, sliced radishes, cilantro and sliced pickles, for serving

1. Light a grill or heat a grill pan. Form the ground pork into four ¾-inch-thick patties, season with salt and grill over moderate heat, turning once, until cooked through, about 8 minutes.

2. In a small bowl, whisk the mayonnaise with the Sriracha and sesame oil; season with salt. Spread the spicy mayonnaise on the buns and top with the burgers, carrot, radishes, cilantro and pickles. Close the burgers and serve.

Beer Fresh, lightly hoppy pilsner.

Crispy Buffalo-Style Potatoes

Warm Potato and Green Bean Salad

Accordion Potatoes, p. 180

Potato-Apple-Dill Pancake, p. 180

Warm Potato and Green Bean Salad

Total **30 min**; Serves **4 to 6**

- ½ cup extra-virgin olive oil
- 3 Tbsp. fresh lemon juice
- 3 Tbsp. Dijon mustard
- ¼ cup chopped tarragon
- 2 Tbsp. minced shallot
- ½ lb. haricots verts or green beans, trimmed
- 3 baking potatoes (2 lbs.), peeled and cut into 1-inch pieces

  Salt and pepper

1. In a large bowl, whisk the olive oil with the lemon juice, mustard, tarragon and shallot. In a medium saucepan of boiling salted water, blanch the green beans for 2 minutes. Using a slotted spoon, transfer the beans to a bowl of ice water to cool; drain and pat dry. Halve the beans and add them to the vinaigrette.

2. Add the potatoes to the boiling water and cook until tender, about 10 minutes. Drain, then add to the vinaigrette. Season with salt and pepper, toss and serve.

Crispy Buffalo-Style Potatoes

Active **15 min**; Total **50 min**
Serves **4 to 6**

- 3 baking potatoes, scrubbed and cut into ½-inch wedges
- 2 Tbsp. extra-virgin olive oil

  Salt and pepper
- 3 Tbsp. unsalted butter, melted
- 2 Tbsp. hot sauce

  Blue cheese dressing, for serving

1. Preheat the oven to 450°. On a rimmed baking sheet, toss the potatoes with the olive oil, season with salt and pepper and roast for 20 minutes. Flip the potatoes and roast for 15 to 20 minutes longer, until golden and crisp.

2. In a large bowl, combine the butter and hot sauce and season with salt and pepper. Add the potatoes and toss to coat. Serve with blue cheese dressing.

Accordion Potatoes

Active **20 min**; Total **1 hr**
Serves **4 to 6**

¼ cup plus 2 Tbsp.
  extra-virgin olive oil

1 Tbsp. smoked paprika

1 lb. new fingerling potatoes

  Salt and pepper

1 bunch of small fresh or
  dried bay leaves

1. Preheat the oven to 375°. In a small bowl, whisk the olive oil with the paprika.

2. Using a sharp paring knife, slice each potato crosswise at ⅛-inch intervals, cutting down but not all the way through the potato. Transfer to a baking sheet. Drizzle with 5 tablespoons of the paprika oil, season with salt and pepper and toss to coat. Roast the potatoes cut side up for 20 minutes. Insert 1 bay leaf into each potato and roast for about 20 minutes longer, until the potatoes are golden, crisp and cooked through. Transfer the potatoes to a platter, discard the bay leaves, drizzle with the remaining tablespoon of paprika oil and serve.

Potato-Apple-Dill Pancakes

Total **25 min**; Makes **12 pancakes**

2 baking potatoes, peeled and
  grated on the large holes
  of a box grater

1 Granny Smith apple, peeled
  and grated on the large holes
  of a box grater

¼ cup chopped dill

3 Tbsp. all-purpose flour

  Salt and pepper

6 Tbsp. canola oil

  Sour cream, for serving

1. Squeeze all the excess water from the potatoes and apples and place them in a bowl. Add the dill and flour, season with salt and pepper and toss to coat thoroughly.

2. In a large nonstick skillet, heat 1 tablespoon of the oil. Spoon ¼ cup of the potato mixture into the skillet for each of 4 pancakes; press gently to flatten. Cook over moderately high heat, turning once and adding 1 tablespoon of oil, until golden and crisp, about 2 minutes per side. Drain briefly on a paper towel–lined plate. Repeat with the remaining potato mixture and oil. Serve with sour cream.

Wine Green apple-inflected sparkling wine, like Spanish cava.

Boiled Potatoes with Sage Butter

Total **30 min**; Serves **4**

- **1** lb. small, round new potatoes
- **4** Tbsp. unsalted butter
- **¼** cup small sage leaves
- **½** lb. breakfast sausage links
- **2** scallions, thinly sliced, plus more for garnish
- **Salt and pepper**

1. In a large saucepan of boiling water, cook the potatoes until tender, about 20 minutes. Drain and halve the potatoes.

2. Meanwhile, in a large nonstick skillet, melt the butter. Add the sage and cook over moderate heat, stirring, for 2 minutes. Pour all but 1 tablespoon of the sage butter into a small bowl. Add the sausages to the skillet and cook over moderate heat until golden and cooked through, 8 to 10 minutes; transfer to a platter.

3. Wipe out the skillet with a paper towel and add the reserved 3 tablespoons of sage butter. Add the 2 scallions and cook over moderate heat, stirring, for 2 minutes. Add the potatoes, season with salt and pepper and stir until warmed through. Top the sausages with the potatoes, garnish with more scallions and serve.

BONUS RECIPE BY CHEF MARIO BATALI

Tortilla Española

Total **45 min**; Serves **6**

- **¼** cup plus 2 Tbsp. extra-virgin olive oil
- **1¼** lbs. Red Bliss potatoes, peeled and sliced ⅛ inch thick
- **1** onion, halved and thinly sliced
- **Kosher salt and pepper**
- **8** large eggs

1. In a large cast-iron skillet, heat ¼ cup of the oil. Add the potato and onion slices, season with salt and pepper and cook over moderate heat, stirring frequently, until the potatoes and onion are tender but not browned, about 15 minutes.

2. In a large bowl, lightly beat the eggs and season with salt and pepper. Scrape the potatoes and onion into the bowl.

3. Preheat the broiler. Return the skillet to the heat; add the remaining 2 tablespoons of oil. Add the egg mixture, spreading it out in an even layer. Cover and cook over low heat until set on the bottom and edge, 10 minutes. Transfer the skillet to the oven and broil 8 inches from the heat just until the top is set, 1 minute longer. Set a large plate over the skillet and carefully invert the *tortilla* onto the plate. Let stand for 5 minutes, cut into wedges and serve warm or at room temperature.

Make Ahead The *tortilla* can stand at room temperature for 3 hours before serving.

Wine Minerally, light-bodied Spanish white, like Albariño.

Quinoa

185   **Quinoa Pilaf with Dates, Olives and Arugula**

185   **Skirt Steak Quinoa Bowls with Ginger-Sesame Dressing**

186   **Quinoa-Dill Omelet with Feta**

187   **Quinoa-Pork Meatballs**

Quinoa Pilaf with Dates,
Olives and Arugula

Quinoa Pilaf with Dates, Olives and Arugula

Total **30 min**; Serves **4**

- **1½ cups white or red quinoa,** rinsed and drained
- **⅓ cup chopped Medjool dates**
- **⅓ cup chopped pitted green olives**
- **1 cup baby arugula**
- **2 Tbsp. extra-virgin olive oil**
- **2 Tbsp. fresh lemon juice**
- **¼ cup sliced scallions**
- **Salt and pepper**

1. In a medium saucepan of boiling water, cook the quinoa until tender, about 10 minutes. Drain and return the quinoa to the pan. Cover and let stand for 10 minutes; fluff with a fork.

2. Transfer the quinoa to a large bowl, add all of the remaining ingredients and season with salt and pepper. Mix well and serve.

Skirt Steak Quinoa Bowls with Ginger-Sesame Dressing

Total **30 min**; Serves **4**

- **1¼ cups white quinoa,** rinsed and drained
- **1 head of Bibb lettuce,** roughly torn
- **2 cups bean sprouts**
- **¼ cup soy sauce**
- **2 Tbsp. finely grated peeled fresh ginger**
- **1 Tbsp. distilled white vinegar**
- **3 Tbsp. toasted sesame oil**
- **1 lb. skirt steak, sliced ¼ inch thick**
- **2 Tbsp. minced garlic**
- **Salt and pepper**

1. In a medium saucepan of boiling water, cook the quinoa until tender, about 10 minutes. Drain and return the quinoa to the pan. Cover and let stand for 10 minutes; fluff with a fork.

2. Divide the quinoa, lettuce and bean sprouts among 4 bowls. In a small bowl, whisk the soy sauce with the ginger, vinegar and 2 tablespoons of the sesame oil.

3. In a large skillet, heat the remaining 1 tablespoon of sesame oil. Add the steak and garlic and cook over high heat, stirring, until the steak is browned, about 2 minutes. Season with salt and pepper. Spoon the steak over the quinoa and serve with the ginger-sesame dressing.

Wine Spiced, medium-bodied Spanish red, like Rioja.

Quinoa-Dill Omelet with Feta

Total **30 min**; Serves **2**

- ¼ **cup red or black quinoa, rinsed and drained**
- 1 **Tbsp. unsalted butter**
- 6 **large eggs**
  Salt
- ¼ **cup crumbled feta cheese**
- 2 **Tbsp. chopped dill**

1. In a medium saucepan of boiling water, cook the quinoa until tender, about 10 minutes. Drain and return the quinoa to the pan. Cover and let stand for 10 minutes; fluff with a fork. Spread on a baking sheet and let cool to room temperature.

2. In a 9-inch nonstick skillet, melt the butter. In a medium bowl, beat the eggs with the quinoa and season with salt. Cook the eggs over moderately low heat, stirring, until almost set, 4 to 5 minutes. Top evenly with the cheese and dill; cook until set. Fold the omelet in half and serve hot.

Wine Fruit-forward sparkling wine, like Prosecco.

Quinoa-Pork Meatballs

Active **20 min**; Total **50 min**; Serves **4**

- ⅓ **cup black or white quinoa, rinsed and drained**
- 1 **lb. ground pork**
- 2 **large eggs, beaten**
- 1 **tsp. kosher salt**
- 1 **tsp. pepper**
- ½ **tsp. freshly grated nutmeg**
- 2 **Tbsp. canola oil**
- 2 **cups jarred marinara sauce**
- 3 **basil sprigs**

1. In a medium saucepan of boiling water, cook the quinoa until tender, about 10 minutes. Drain and return the quinoa to the pan. Cover and let stand for 10 minutes; fluff with a fork. Spread the quinoa on a baking sheet and let cool to room temperature.

2. In a large bowl, combine the quinoa, pork, eggs, salt, pepper and nutmeg. Mix well and form into 12 meatballs.

3. In a large cast-iron skillet, heat the oil. Add the meatballs and cook over moderate heat, turning, until browned, about 8 minutes. Stir in the marinara sauce and basil and bring to a simmer. Cover and cook over low heat until the meatballs are cooked through, 7 to 8 minutes, then serve.

Wine Earthy, medium-bodied red, like Pinot Noir.

Rice

191   **Coconut Rice Salad**

191   **Baked Shrimp Risotto**

192   **Indian Fried Rice with Chickpeas and Spinach**

192   **Spiced Rice Breakfast Porridge**

193   **Rice Pudding Brûlée**

Coconut Rice Salad

Baked Shrimp Risotto

Indian Fried Rice with
Chickpeas and Spinach, p. 192

Spiced Rice Breakfast
Porridge, p. 192

Coconut Rice Salad

Active **10 min**; Total **40 min**; Serves **4**

- 1 **cup jasmine rice**
- 2 **cups unsweetened coconut milk**
- 1 **Tbsp. sugar**
  Kosher salt
- 2 **cups shredded cooked chicken**
- 2 **small Kirby cucumbers, chopped**
- 1 **Tbsp. canola oil**
  Chopped scallions, for garnish

1. In a large saucepan, combine the rice, coconut milk, sugar and ½ teaspoon of salt and bring to a boil. Cover and cook over low heat until the rice is tender and all of the coconut milk is absorbed, about 20 minutes. Remove from the heat and let the rice stand, covered, for 10 minutes.

2. Transfer the rice to a large bowl and stir in the chicken, cucumbers and oil. Season with salt, garnish with scallions and serve.

Wine Zesty, medium-bodied white, like Australian Riesling.

Baked Shrimp Risotto

Active **10 min**; Total **30 min**; Serves **4**

- 2 **Tbsp. extra-virgin olive oil**
- 5 **garlic cloves, thinly sliced**
- 1 **cup arborio rice**
- 3½ **cups low-sodium chicken broth**
- ½ **cup freshly grated Parmigiano-Reggiano cheese, plus more for garnish**
- 20 **cooked shelled large shrimp**
- 1 **Tbsp. unsalted butter**
- 1 **Tbsp. fresh lemon juice**
  Salt
  Pesto, for serving

1. Preheat the oven to 400°. In a medium enameled cast-iron casserole, heat the olive oil. Add the garlic and rice and cook over moderate heat, stirring, until very fragrant, 2 minutes. Stir in the broth and bring to a boil.

2. Cover the casserole and bake for about 20 minutes, until the rice is tender. Stir in the ½ cup of cheese along with the shrimp, butter and lemon juice; season with salt. Serve, drizzled with pesto and garnished with cheese.

Wine Lemony coastal Italian white, like Vermentino.

Indian Fried Rice with Chickpeas and Spinach

Total **20 min**; Serves **4**

- 3 Tbsp. canola oil
- 1 shallot, thinly sliced
- 1 Tbsp. minced peeled fresh ginger
- 1 tsp. cumin seeds
- 4 cups steamed basmati rice
  One 14½-oz. can chickpeas, rinsed
- 4 cups curly spinach
  Salt and pepper
  Lemon wedges, for serving

In a large nonstick skillet, heat the oil. Add the shallot and ginger and cook over moderate heat, stirring occasionally, until the shallot is golden, about 3 minutes. Add the cumin, rice, chickpeas and spinach and cook, stirring, until the spinach is wilted, about 3 minutes. Season with salt and pepper. Serve with lemon wedges.

Wine Peach-inflected, spicy Rhône white.

Spiced Rice Breakfast Porridge

Active **10 min**; Total **40 min**; Serves **4**

- 1 cup steel-cut oats (not quick-cooking)
- ½ cup short-grain brown rice (not quick-cooking)
  One 3-inch cinnamon stick
- ⅓ cup plus 2 Tbsp. turbinado sugar
- ½ tsp. kosher salt
- 2 Tbsp. unsalted butter
- 2 bananas, peeled and halved lengthwise
  Chopped roasted almonds and heavy cream, for serving

1. In a medium saucepan, combine 4 cups of water with the oats, rice, cinnamon stick, ⅓ cup of the sugar and the salt; bring to a simmer. Cover and cook over low heat, stirring occasionally, until tender and thickened, about 30 minutes. Discard the cinnamon stick.

2. Meanwhile, in a nonstick skillet, melt the butter. Press the remaining 2 tablespoons of sugar on the cut sides of the bananas. Cook sugar side down over moderately high heat until caramelized, about 2 minutes. Top the porridge with the bananas. Serve with chopped almonds and cream.

Rice Pudding Brûlée

Active **1 hr**; Total **2 hr**
Serves **6**

- 6 **cups whole milk**
- **Zest of 1 lemon, in wide strips**
- 1 **cinnamon stick, broken in half**
- 1 **cup medium-grain rice (7 oz.), such as Bomba, Valencia or arborio**
- ³/₄ **cup heavy cream**
- ½ **cup granulated sugar**
- 6 **Tbsp. light brown sugar**

1. In a medium enameled cast-iron casserole, combine the milk with the lemon zest and cinnamon stick and bring to a simmer over moderate heat. Add the rice and cook over low heat for 20 minutes, stirring occasionally. Discard the lemon zest and cinnamon stick. Continue to cook the rice, stirring often, until it is just tender, about 50 minutes. Add the cream and simmer, stirring often, until the rice is very tender and the pudding is creamy, about 15 minutes.

2. Stir in the granulated sugar and simmer over moderate heat until dissolved, about 2 minutes. Spoon the pudding into six 1-cup ramekins and let cool to room temperature, about 30 minutes.

3. Preheat the broiler. Using a coarse sieve, sift 1 tablespoon of brown sugar over each pudding. Set 3 ramekins on a small baking sheet and broil 4 inches from the heat for 20 seconds, until the sugar is bubbling; repeat with the remaining ramekins. Let cool until the sugar hardens, then serve.

Make Ahead The pudding can be refrigerated for up to 2 days. Top with brown sugar and broil just before serving.

Salmon

197 Salmon and Citrus Salad with Poppy Seed Dressing

197 Salmon, Broccolini and Fresh Red Chile Papillotes

198 Salmon and Cherry Tomato Skewers with Rosemary Vinaigrette

198 Salmon Sandwiches with Bacon and Apple-Horseradish Mayo

Sausage

200 Sausage and Cheddar Muffins

201 Sausage Choucroute

202 Sausage and Fennel Parm Heroes

203 Warm Escarole Salad with Sausage Vinaigrette

Shrimp

204 Shrimp and Chorizo Tortas

204 Shrimp Salad with Green Curry Dressing

206 Shrimp Cakes with Spicy Mayo

206 Angry Shrimp Spaghettini

207 Grilled Shrimp with Shrimp Butter

Snap Peas

208 Double-Pea Sauté with Ground Pork

209 Warm Snap Peas with Ham and Tarragon Butter

211 Snap Pea and Radish Salad with Tahini Dressing

211 Snap Pea Falafel Salad

Spinach

213 Quinoa with Spinach and Roasted Almonds

213 Spinach and Caramelized Onion Dip

214 Spinach Salad with Walnut Vinaigrette

214 Asian Pork Noodles with Spinach

215 Spinach Spoon Bread

Strawberries

216 Caramelized Panzanella with Strawberries

217 Strawberry-Prosecco Gelées

218 Strawberry Shortcake

219 Fresh Strawberry Sauce

219 Balsamic Strawberries with Strawberry Sorbet

Sweet Potatoes

220 Sweet Potato Hash Browns

220 Sweet Potato-Tomato Pasta Sauce

222 Sweet Potatoes with Almond Pesto

222 Sweet Potato and Mushroom Salad

223 Baked Sweet Potato Chips

**Salmon and Citrus Salad
with Poppy Seed Dressing**

Salmon and Citrus Salad with Poppy Seed Dressing

Total **45 min**; Serves **4 to 6**

- 1 lb. salmon fillet

  Salt and pepper
- ½ cup buttermilk
- 2 Tbsp. extra-virgin olive oil
- 1½ tsp. poppy seeds
- 2 medium navel oranges, such as Cara Cara, peeled and sliced ½ inch thick or separated into sections
- 1 medium grapefruit, peeled, sections cut into thirds
- 1 Hass avocado, sliced into wedges

  Snipped chives, for garnish

1. Preheat the oven to 375°. Lay the salmon fillet skin side down on a rimmed baking sheet and season with salt and pepper. Bake for about 20 minutes, until just cooked through. Let cool, then flake into large chunks; discard the skin.

2. Meanwhile, in a small bowl, whisk the buttermilk with the olive oil and poppy seeds. Season the dressing with salt and pepper.

3. Arrange the salmon, oranges, grapefruit and avocado on a platter or plates. Drizzle some of the dressing on top. Garnish with snipped chives and serve, passing additional dressing at the table.

Wine Vibrant, medium-bodied Spanish white, like Verdejo.

Salmon, Broccolini and Fresh Red Chile Papillotes

Active **15 min**; Total **30 min**; Serves **4**

- 1 lb. Broccolini

  Four 6-oz. skinless center-cut salmon fillets
- 8 thin slices of lemon
- 1 Fresno chile, thinly sliced into rings
- 6 Tbsp. extra-virgin olive oil

  Salt and pepper

1. Preheat the oven to 425°. Lay 4 large sheets of parchment paper on a work surface. Divide the Broccolini among the parchment sheets and top each mound with a salmon fillet, 2 lemon slices and some chile rings; drizzle each fillet with 1½ tablespoons of olive oil and season with salt and pepper. Fold the parchment over the fish, then fold the edge over itself in small pleats to seal the papillotes.

2. Transfer the papillotes to a large baking sheet and bake for 15 minutes, until slightly puffed. Carefully snip the packets open with scissors and serve.

Wine Crisp, white peach–scented northern Italian white, like Müller-Thurgau.

Salmon and Cherry Tomato Skewers with Rosemary Vinaigrette

Total **40 min**; Serves **4**

¼ cup extra-virgin olive oil, plus more for brushing

3 Tbsp. fresh lemon juice

2 tsp. Dijon mustard

2 tsp. finely chopped rosemary

Salt and pepper

1½ lbs. skinless salmon fillet, cut into 1½-inch cubes

16 cherry tomatoes

4 long metal skewers, or wooden skewers soaked in water for 1 hour

1. In a small bowl, whisk the ¼ cup of olive oil with the lemon juice, mustard and rosemary. Season the vinaigrette with salt and pepper.

2. Light a grill or heat a grill pan. Thread the salmon and cherry tomatoes onto the skewers, brush with olive oil and season all over with salt and pepper. Grill over moderately high heat, turning once, until the salmon is just cooked through, about 6 minutes. Transfer the skewers to a platter and drizzle with some of the vinaigrette. Serve right away, passing additional vinaigrette at the table.

Wine Juicy, lively Oregon Chardonnay.

Salmon Sandwiches with Bacon and Apple-Horseradish Mayo

Total **40 min**; Serves **4**

½ cup mayonnaise

½ cup finely chopped Granny Smith apple

3 Tbsp. drained prepared horseradish

Salt and pepper

8 slices of bacon

1 Tbsp. canola oil

Four 5- to 6-oz. skinless center-cut salmon fillets

4 brioche burger buns, split and toasted

4 lettuce leaves

1. In a small bowl, whisk the mayonnaise with the apple and horseradish. Season the mayo with salt and pepper.

2. In a large nonstick skillet, cook the bacon over moderate heat, turning occasionally, until browned and crisp, 5 to 7 minutes. Transfer to paper towels to drain.

3. Wipe out the skillet and heat the oil in it. Season the salmon with salt and pepper and cook over moderately high heat, turning once, until just cooked through, 6 to 8 minutes.

4. Spread the apple-horseradish mayonnaise on the buns and top with the salmon, bacon and lettuce. Close the sandwiches and serve.

Wine Dark cherry–rich, medium-bodied Pinot Noir, like one from Sonoma.

Salmon and Cherry
Tomato Skewers with
Rosemary Vinaigrette

Sausage and Cheddar Muffins

Active **10 min**; Total **40 min**
Makes **12 muffins**

- 2 **cups all-purpose flour**
- 1 **Tbsp. baking powder**
- ¾ **tsp. kosher salt**
- ½ **tsp. baking soda**
- 4 **Tbsp. unsalted butter, melted**
- 1 **large egg, beaten**
- 1 **cup whole milk**
- 1 **cup shredded sharp cheddar cheese**
- 1 **cup chopped cooked breakfast sausage**

Preheat the oven to 375°. In a large bowl, whisk the flour with the baking powder, salt and baking soda. Stir in the butter, egg, milk, cheese and sausage. Spoon the batter into 12 greased muffin cups and bake for 25 to 30 minutes, until golden. Transfer to a rack to cool before serving.

Make Ahead The muffins can be refrigerated overnight. Reheat in a 350° oven for about 10 minutes before serving.

Sausage Choucroute

Active **10 min**; Total **55 min**; Serves **4**

- 1 lb. mixed sausages, such as bratwurst and fresh chorizo
- 1 lb. small Yukon Gold potatoes, quartered

  One 25-oz. jar sauerkraut, drained (3 cups)
- 2 Tbsp. extra-virgin olive oil
- 1 tsp. caraway seeds

  Salt and pepper

  Crusty bread and grainy mustard, for serving

Preheat the oven to 425°. In a large cast-iron skillet, toss the sausages with the potatoes, sauerkraut, olive oil and caraway seeds; season with salt and pepper. Roast until the potatoes are golden and cooked through, about 45 minutes. Serve the sausage choucroute with crusty bread and mustard.

Wine Ripe, lightly off-dry Alsace Riesling.

Sausage and Fennel Parm Heroes

Total **30 min**; Serves **4**

- **4** hoagie rolls, split
- **2** Tbsp. extra-virgin olive oil
- **1** lb. sweet Italian sausage
- **3** fennel bulbs–halved, cored and thinly sliced (4 cups)
- Salt and pepper
- **1½** cups jarred marinara sauce
- **8** oz. fresh mozzarella, sliced
- Basil leaves, for garnish

1. Preheat the broiler. Place the rolls cut side up on a baking sheet. In a large skillet, heat the olive oil. Add the sausage and fennel and season with salt and pepper. Cook over moderate heat, stirring occasionally, until the fennel is deep golden and the sausage is cooked through, 12 to 15 minutes.

2. Mound the mixture on the bottom halves of the rolls, then top with the marinara and mozzarella. Broil 6 inches from the heat until the cheese is melted, about 3 minutes. Top with the basil, close the sandwiches and serve.

Beer Fresh, mild Italian lager.

Warm Escarole Salad with Sausage Vinaigrette

Total **25 min**; Serves **4**

- 2 Tbsp. extra-virgin olive oil
- 6 oz. hot Italian sausage, casing removed, meat crumbled
- 3 oil-packed anchovy fillets, drained
- 1 Tbsp. drained capers
- 2 Tbsp. fresh lemon juice
- 3 radishes, thinly sliced
- 1 head of escarole (12 oz.), leaves torn into bite-size pieces (8 cups)

  Salt and pepper
- 2 Tbsp. chopped tarragon

In a large skillet, heat the olive oil. Add the sausage, anchovies and capers and cook over moderate heat, stirring to break up the meat, until cooked through, about 5 minutes. Add the lemon juice, radishes and escarole and stir until the escarole is wilted; season with salt and pepper. Transfer to a platter, garnish with the tarragon and serve.

Wine Tangy, fruit-forward Sauvignon Blanc.

Shrimp and Chorizo Tortas

Total **30 min**; Serves **4**

- 2 Tbsp. canola oil
- ¾ lb. shelled and deveined medium shrimp
- ½ lb. fresh chorizo, casing removed, meat crumbled
- ¾ cup finely chopped red onion
- 1 garlic clove, minced
- 2 Tbsp. fresh lime juice

  Salt and pepper

  Toasted kaiser rolls, mayonnaise, lettuce and thinly sliced tomato and avocado, for serving

In a large skillet, heat the oil. Add the shrimp, chorizo, onion and garlic and cook over high heat, stirring occasionally, until browned and the shrimp and chorizo are cooked through, about 8 minutes. Stir in the lime juice and 2 tablespoons of water and season with salt and pepper. Serve on toasted kaiser rolls with mayonnaise, lettuce and sliced tomato and avocado.

Wine Robust, full-bodied rosé.

Shrimp Salad with Green Curry Dressing

Total **30 min**; Serves **4 to 6**

- ¼ cup fresh lime juice
- ¼ cup canola oil
- 2 Tbsp. green curry paste
- 1 lb. cooked large shrimp
- 8 oz. mixed torn lettuces (about 10 cups)
- 1 cup cilantro leaves
- 1 cup mint leaves
- 1 cup thinly sliced carrot
- ½ cup thinly sliced red onion

  Salt

  Chopped roasted peanuts, for garnish

In a large bowl, whisk the lime juice with the canola oil and green curry paste. Add the shrimp, lettuce, herbs and vegetables and toss well. Season with salt and toss again. Garnish with chopped peanuts and serve right away.

Wine Full-bodied, pear-scented California Chardonnay.

Shrimp and Chorizo Tortas

Shrimp Salad with Green Curry Dressing

Shrimp Cakes
with Spicy
Mayo, p. 206

Angry Shrimp Spaghettini, p. 206

Shrimp Cakes with Spicy Mayo

Total **30 min**; Serves **4**

- ½ **cup mayonnaise**
- 1 **Tbsp. hot sauce**
- 1 **lb. shelled and deveined shrimp, chopped**
- ¾ **cup panko**
- 2 **large eggs**
- 3 **Tbsp. finely chopped scallions**
- 1 **tsp. finely grated lemon zest**
- ¾ **tsp. smoked paprika**
- 1 **tsp. salt**
- ½ **tsp. pepper**
- ¼ **cup extra-virgin olive oil**
  Lemon wedges, for serving

1. In a small bowl, whisk the mayonnaise with the hot sauce.

2. In a large bowl, mix the chopped shrimp with the panko, eggs, scallions, lemon zest, smoked paprika, salt and pepper. Form the mixture into eight ¾-inch-thick cakes.

3. In a large skillet, heat the olive oil. In batches, add the cakes and cook over moderately high heat, turning once, until browned and cooked through, about 4 minutes. Transfer to plates and serve with the spicy mayonnaise and lemon wedges.

Wine Spritzy, citrusy Vinho Verde.

Angry Shrimp Spaghettini

Total **30 min**; Serves **4 to 6**

- 1 **lb. spaghettini**
- ½ **cup extra-virgin olive oil**
- 1 **lb. shelled and deveined large shrimp**
- ½ **cup panko**
- 2 **tsp. crushed red pepper**
- 2 **garlic cloves, thinly sliced**
- 1 **tsp. finely grated lemon zest**
  Salt and pepper
  Chopped parsley, for garnish

1. In a pot of salted boiling water, cook the pasta until al dente. Drain, reserving 1 cup of the cooking water.

2. In a large saucepan, heat the olive oil. Add the shrimp, panko, crushed red pepper, garlic and lemon zest. Season with salt and pepper and cook over moderately high heat, stirring occasionally, until the shrimp are just cooked through, about 6 minutes.

3. Add the pasta and reserved cooking water to the skillet and cook, tossing, until coated, about 2 minutes. Transfer to shallow bowls, garnish with chopped parsley and serve.

Wine Full-bodied, slightly off-dry Chenin Blanc, like Vouvray.

Grilled Shrimp with Shrimp Butter

Total **30 min**; Serves **6**

- 6 Tbsp. unsalted butter
- ½ cup finely chopped red onion
- 1½ tsp. crushed red pepper
- 1 tsp. Malaysian shrimp paste (belacan; see Note)
- 1½ tsp. fresh lime juice

  Salt
- 24 large shrimp, shelled and deveined

  Black pepper
- 6 long wooden skewers, soaked in water for 30 minutes

  Torn mint leaves and assorted sprouts, for garnish

1. In a small skillet, melt 3 tablespoons of the butter. Add the onion and cook over moderate heat until softened, about 3 minutes. Whisk in the crushed red pepper and shrimp paste and cook, stirring, until fragrant, 2 minutes. Whisk in the lime juice and the remaining 3 tablespoons of butter and season with salt. Keep the shrimp butter warm.

2. Light a grill or heat a grill pan. Season the shrimp with salt and black pepper and thread onto the skewers (don't pack them on too tightly). Grill over high heat, turning once, until lightly charred and just cooked through, about 4 minutes. Transfer to a platter and spoon the shrimp butter on top. Garnish with mint leaves and sprouts and serve.

Note Belacan is a pungent seasoning made by grinding small shrimp into a paste that is fermented, dried and pressed into cakes. It's available at Southeast Asian markets or online from *indomart.us.*

Make Ahead The shrimp butter can be refrigerated overnight. Warm gently over low heat before serving.

Beer Citrusy farmhouse ale.

Double-Pea Sauté with Ground Pork

Total **30 min**; Serves **4 to 6**

- **2 Tbsp. canola oil**
- **½ lb. ground pork**
- **2 Tbsp. finely chopped peeled fresh ginger**
- **2 Tbsp. finely chopped garlic**
- **½ lb. snap peas**
- **½ lb. fresh shelled or thawed frozen peas**
- **2 Tbsp. fresh lime juice**
- **1 cup chopped basil**
- **Salt and pepper**

In a large nonstick skillet, heat the oil. Add the pork, ginger and garlic and stir-fry over moderately high heat until the pork is browned, about 2 minutes. Stir in the snap peas and shelled peas and stir-fry until crisp-tender, about 3 minutes. Stir in the lime juice and basil, season with salt and pepper and serve.

Wine Medium-bodied, herb-scented white, like Grüner Veltliner.

Warm Snap Peas with Ham and Tarragon Butter

Total **20 min**; Serves **4 to 6**

- ½ lb. snap peas, halved lengthwise
- ½ lb. cooked ham, shredded
- 3 Tbsp. unsalted butter, at room temperature
- 3 Tbsp. chopped tarragon
- 1 Tbsp. fresh lemon juice
- Salt and pepper

In a steamer basket set over a saucepan of simmering water, steam the snap peas and ham until the peas are crisp-tender, about 3 minutes. Transfer to a large bowl and add the butter, tarragon and lemon juice. Season with salt and pepper, mix well and serve.

Wine Crisp, savory Spanish white, like Albariño.

Snap Pea and Radish Salad
with Tahini Dressing

Snap Pea and Radish Salad with Tahini Dressing

Total **20 min**; Serves **4 to 6**

- ⅓ cup extra-virgin olive oil
- ⅓ cup tahini
- 2 Tbsp. fresh lemon juice
- 1 Tbsp. toasted sesame seeds
- ½ lb. snap peas, thinly sliced
- ½ lb. radishes, thinly sliced
- 2 cups mixed chopped herbs, such as parsley, mint and chives
- Salt and pepper

In a large bowl, whisk the olive oil with the tahini, lemon juice, sesame seeds and 2 tablespoons of water. Add the snap peas, radishes and herbs and season with salt and pepper. Mix well and serve.

Snap Pea Falafel Salad

Total **20 min**; Serves **4 to 6**

- ¼ cup extra-virgin olive oil
- 2 Tbsp. fresh lemon juice
- 1 tsp. cumin seeds, crushed
- 1 garlic clove, minced
- 3 cups cooked bulgur
- ½ lb. snap peas, chopped
- 1 tomato, chopped
- 2 scallions, thinly sliced
- 1 cup canned chickpeas
- ⅓ cup chopped parsley
- Salt and pepper

In a large bowl, whisk the olive oil with the lemon juice, cumin seeds and garlic. Add the bulgur, snap peas, tomato, scallions, chickpeas and parsley and season with salt and pepper. Mix well and serve.

Quinoa with Spinach and
Roasted Almonds

Spinach and Caramelized Onion Dip

Asian Pork Noodles with Spinach, p. 214

Spinach Salad with
Walnut Vinaigrette,
p. 214

Quinoa with Spinach and Roasted Almonds

Total **40 min**; Serves **6**

1⅓ cups quinoa,
   rinsed and drained

 8 oz. curly spinach
   (8 packed cups), stemmed
   and finely chopped (4 cups)

 3 radishes, thinly sliced

 6 Tbsp. extra-virgin olive oil

 2 Tbsp. fresh lemon juice

   Salt and pepper

½ cup chopped roasted almonds

1. In a medium saucepan of boiling water, cook the quinoa until tender, about 10 minutes. Drain and return the quinoa to the pan. Cover and let stand for 10 minutes; fluff with a fork.

2. In a large bowl, toss the quinoa with the spinach, radishes, olive oil and lemon juice. Season with salt and pepper and toss again. Garnish with the almonds and serve.

Make Ahead The recipe can be kept at room temperature for up to 3 hours.

Spinach and Caramelized Onion Dip

Total **30 min**; Makes **2 cups**

 3 Tbsp. extra-virgin olive oil

 1 large onion, thinly sliced

 4 oz. curly spinach (4 packed
   cups), stemmed

 1 cup nonfat Greek yogurt

¼ cup chopped chives

½ tsp. freshly grated nutmeg

   Salt and pepper

   Crackers, for serving

1. In a large nonstick skillet, heat 2 tablespoons of the olive oil. Add the onion and cook over moderate heat, stirring occasionally, until deeply golden, about 15 minutes. Stir in the remaining 1 tablespoon of oil and the spinach and stir until wilted. Transfer to a medium bowl and let cool to room temperature.

2. Stir the yogurt, chives and nutmeg into the spinach and onion and season the dip with salt and pepper. Serve with crackers.

Make Ahead The dip can be refrigerated overnight.

Spinach Salad with Walnut Vinaigrette

Total **25 min**; Serves **6**

1 cup walnuts, finely chopped

8 oz. curly spinach
(8 packed cups)

4 oz. white mushrooms, sliced

1 Hass avocado, sliced

¼ cup extra-virgin olive oil

¼ cup apple cider vinegar

Salt and pepper

In a small skillet, toast the walnuts over low heat, stirring, until golden, 6 to 8 minutes. Transfer to a large bowl and let cool. Add the spinach, mushrooms, avocado, oil and vinegar. Season with salt and pepper, toss to coat and serve.

Asian Pork Noodles with Spinach

Total **25 min**; Serves **4**

12 oz. spaghetti, broken into
3-inch pieces

2 Tbsp. canola oil

1 lb. ground pork

3 Tbsp. finely chopped garlic

3 Tbsp. finely chopped peeled
fresh ginger

2 Tbsp. Asian fish sauce

2 Tbsp. fresh lime juice

8 oz. curly spinach
(8 packed cups)

Salt and pepper

Chopped basil, for garnish

1. In a pot of salted boiling water, cook the spaghetti until al dente. Drain.

2. In a large skillet, heat the oil. Add the pork, garlic and ginger and cook over moderate heat, stirring, until browned, about 5 minutes. Stir in the pasta, fish sauce, lime juice and spinach; season with salt and pepper and toss well. Transfer to bowls, garnish with basil and serve.

Wine Ripe, fruit-forward, dry German Riesling.

Spinach Spoon Bread

Active **15 min**; Total **1 hr**
Serves **12**

 3 **Tbsp. unsalted butter, melted, plus more for greasing**

10 **oz. baby spinach**

 3 **cups buttermilk**

 3 **large eggs, separated**

 1 **cup medium-grind yellow cornmeal**

¼ **cup plus 2 Tbsp. all-purpose flour**

 1 **Tbsp. sugar**

1½ **tsp. baking soda**

   Scant 1 tsp. kosher salt

   Pinch of freshly grated nutmeg

   Pinch of freshly ground white pepper

1. Preheat the oven to 350° and butter a 9-by-13-inch baking dish or very large enameled cast-iron skillet. In a saucepan of boiling water, cook the spinach just until wilted, about 30 seconds. Drain and cool under running water, then squeeze out as much water as possible. Finely chop the spinach.

2. In a large bowl, whisk the buttermilk with the egg yolks, cornmeal, flour, sugar, baking soda, salt, nutmeg, white pepper and the 3 tablespoons of melted butter. Fold in the chopped spinach.

3. In a clean bowl, using a handheld electric mixer, beat the egg whites until soft peaks form. Fold the whites into the batter and scrape it into the prepared baking dish.

4. Bake the spoon bread in the center of the oven for about 45 minutes, until golden. Let cool slightly, then serve.

Make Ahead The spoon bread can be made earlier in the day and kept at room temperature; reheat in a 325° oven.

Caramelized Panzanella with Strawberries

Total **25 min**; Serves 4

4 Tbsp. unsalted butter

7 oz. sourdough bread, crusts removed, bread torn into 2-inch chunks (about 2 cups)

¼ cup sugar

¼ tsp. cinnamon

¼ tsp. ground cardamom

½ tsp. kosher salt

12 oz. strawberries, halved (2 heaping cups)

Whipped cream and chopped pistachios, for serving

1. In a large skillet, heat the butter. Add the bread, sugar, cinnamon, cardamom and salt and cook over high heat, tossing often, until the bread is caramelized all over, 3 to 4 minutes.

2. Transfer the bread to plates and top with the strawberries and a dollop of whipped cream. Sprinkle with chopped pistachios and serve.

Strawberry-Prosecco Gelées

Total **15 min plus 4 hr chilling**
Serves **4**

1½ tsp. unflavored
    powdered gelatin

 2 cups chilled Prosecco

¼ cup sugar

 1 cup chopped strawberries

1. In a small saucepan, stir the gelatin with ½ cup of the Prosecco and let stand for 5 minutes. Add the sugar and cook over low heat, stirring, until the gelatin and sugar dissolve.

2. Pour the gelée mixture into a large glass measuring cup and add the remaining 1½ cups of Prosecco. Spoon the strawberries into coupes or flutes and top with the Prosecco gelée. Refrigerate until set, at least 4 hours, then serve.

Make Ahead The gelées can be refrigerated overnight.

Strawberry Shortcake

Active **30 min**; Total **1 hr plus cooling**; Serves **8**

1½ **sticks cold unsalted butter, cubed, plus more for greasing**

2 **cups self-rising flour, plus more for dusting**

¼ **cup sugar**

2 **cups chilled heavy cream**

8 **oz. strawberries, quartered (1½ cups)**

1. Preheat the oven to 425°. Butter and flour an 8-inch round cake pan. In a large bowl, mix the 2 cups of flour with the sugar. Cut or rub in the 1½ sticks of butter until pea-size crumbs form. Using a fork, stir in 1 cup of the cream until a dough forms. Scrape the dough into the prepared pan and lightly press it over the bottom.

2. Bake the cake for 30 minutes, until golden and a toothpick inserted in the center comes out clean. Transfer to a rack and let cool for 10 minutes, then unmold and let cool completely.

3. In a medium bowl, whisk the remaining 1 cup of cream until stiff peaks form. Cut the cake in half horizontally. Spread the bottom layer with the strawberries followed by the whipped cream. Cover with the top cake layer and serve immediately.

Fresh Strawberry Sauce

Total **5 min**; Makes **1 cup**

 1 **cup chopped strawberries**

¼ **cup packed light brown sugar**

 2 **Tbsp. fresh grapefruit juice**

¼ **tsp. ground ginger**

¼ **tsp. kosher salt**

   Vanilla ice cream, for serving

In a medium bowl, mash the strawberries with the brown sugar, grapefruit juice, ginger and salt until the sugar dissolves. Serve over vanilla ice cream.

BONUS RECIPE BY CHEF MARIO BATALI

Balsamic Strawberries with Strawberry Sorbet

Active **10 min**; Total **40 min**
Serves **6**

 1 **lb. strawberries, quartered**

1½ **Tbsp. good-quality balsamic vinegar**

   Freshly ground pepper

   Strawberry sorbet, for serving

In a large bowl, toss the strawberries with the vinegar and a generous pinch of pepper. Let stand at room temperature for 30 minutes. Serve over strawberry sorbet.

Sweet Potato Hash Browns

Total **45 min**; Serves **4**

- 3 poblano chiles
- 2 Tbsp. extra-virgin olive oil
- 1 small red onion, thinly sliced
- 2 Tbsp. unsalted butter
- 2 medium sweet potatoes (1½ lbs.), peeled and cut into ¼-inch dice
- 3 garlic cloves, thinly sliced
- 1 rosemary sprig
- 2 Tbsp. fresh lemon juice
- Salt and pepper

1. Roast the poblanos directly over a gas flame or under a preheated broiler, turning, until charred all over. Transfer to a bowl, cover tightly with plastic wrap and let cool. Peel, seed and stem the poblanos, then thinly slice them.

2. In a large skillet, heat the olive oil. Add the onion and cook, stirring, until golden, about 5 minutes. Add the butter, sweet potatoes, garlic and rosemary and cook over moderate heat, stirring occasionally, until the potatoes are tender and lightly browned, about 10 minutes. Stir in the poblanos and lemon juice and season with salt and pepper. Discard the rosemary sprig and serve the hash browns.

Serve With Fried eggs.

Sweet Potato–Tomato Pasta Sauce

Total **30 min**; Makes **3 cups**

- 1 large sweet potato (1 lb.), peeled and cut into 2-inch pieces
- 1 large tomato (8 oz.), chopped
- ¼ cup heavy cream
- 2 Tbsp. extra-virgin olive oil
- Salt and pepper

Place the sweet potato in a large saucepan and add enough water to cover by 2 inches. Boil until tender, about 20 minutes. Drain and transfer the sweet potato to a blender. Add the tomato, cream, olive oil and ½ cup of water and puree until smooth. Season the sauce with salt and pepper.

Make Ahead The sauce can be refrigerated for up to 1 week or frozen for 1 month.

Sweet Potato Hash Browns

Sweet Potato–Tomato Sauce
with Spaghetti

Sweet Potatoes with
Almond Pesto, p. 222

Sweet Potato and Mushroom Salad, p. 222

Sweet Potatoes with Almond Pesto

Total **40 min**; Serves **6 to 8**

2 **medium sweet potatoes (1½ lbs.), scrubbed and cut into ½-inch-thick wedges**

¾ **cup plus 2 Tbsp. extra-virgin olive oil**

Salt and pepper

1 **cup sliced almonds**

1 **packed cup basil leaves**

1 **small garlic clove, crushed**

¼ **cup freshly grated Parmigiano-Reggiano cheese**

2 **Tbsp. fresh lemon juice**

1. Preheat the oven to 425°. On a baking sheet, toss the sweet potatoes with 2 tablespoons of the olive oil and season with salt and pepper. Roast for 25 to 30 minutes, turning occasionally, until tender and golden brown.

2. Meanwhile, in a pie plate, toast the almonds for about 3 minutes, until lightly golden; let cool completely. In a food processor, pulse the almonds with the basil and garlic until finely chopped. With the machine on, drizzle in the remaining ¾ cup of olive oil. Transfer the pesto to a small bowl, stir in the cheese and lemon juice and season with salt and pepper. Serve the roasted sweet potatoes with the pesto.

Make Ahead The pesto can be refrigerated overnight.

Sweet Potato and Mushroom Salad

Total **45 min**; Serves **4 to 6**

2 **Tbsp. white miso**

2 **Tbsp. Dijon mustard**

¼ **cup plus 3 Tbsp. canola oil**

½ **lb. wild mushrooms, coarsely chopped**

2 **medium sweet potatoes (1½ lbs.), preferably Japanese white, scrubbed and cut into 1½-inch pieces**

Salt and pepper

Chopped chives, for garnish

1. Preheat the oven to 425°. In a small bowl, whisk the miso with the mustard, ¼ cup of the canola oil and 2 tablespoons of water.

2. In a large bowl, toss the mushrooms and sweet potatoes with the remaining 3 tablespoons of canola oil and season with salt and pepper. Spread the potatoes on a baking sheet and roast for 15 minutes. Turn the potatoes and add the mushrooms. Roast for 10 minutes longer, until the potatoes are tender and golden and the mushrooms are browned. Transfer the potatoes and mushrooms to a platter and drizzle with the dressing. Garnish with chives and serve warm.

Make Ahead The dressing can be refrigerated for up to 1 week.

Baked Sweet Potato Chips

Active **10 min**; Total **1 hr 15 min**
Makes **3 cups**

- 1 **small sweet potato (8 oz.),
  peeled and sliced on a
  mandoline** ⅛ **inch thick**
- 3 **Tbsp. extra-virgin olive oil**

  Salt and pepper

Preheat the oven to 275°. Set a rack on each of 2 baking
sheets. In a large bowl, toss the sweet potato slices with the
olive oil and season with salt and pepper; make sure each
slice is coated with oil. Arrange the slices in a single layer
on the racks. Bake for 45 to 50 minutes, rotating the sheets
halfway through baking, until the chips are deeply golden.
The chips will crisp up as they cool.

Make Ahead The chips can be stored in an airtight container
overnight. Recrisp in a 250° oven if necessary.

Tofu

227 **Creamy Sesame-Garlic Tofu Dressing**

227 **Seared Tofu Tabbouleh**

228 **Crispy Tofu Steaks with Ginger Vinaigrette**

229 **Tofu Masala**

Tomatoes

230 **Summery Fresh Tomato Soup**

230 **Roasted Tomatoes with Anchovies and Capers**

232 **Pappardelle with Tomatoes, Almonds and Parmesan**

233 **Tomato Salad with Horseradish Ranch Dressing**

234 **Garlic-Toasted Tomato Tartines**

234 **Garlicky Cherry Tomato and Bread Gratin**

Turkey

237 **Turkey Tonnato**

237 **Turkey Curry Soup**

238 **Turkey-Stuffing Salad**

238 **Turkey Reuben Hash**

239 **Turkey and Pinto Bean Chili**

Creamy Sesame-
Garlic Tofu Dressing

Creamy Sesame-Garlic Tofu Dressing

Total **10 min**; Makes **1¼ cups**

- 8 oz. silken tofu, drained
- ¼ cup toasted sesame seeds
- ¼ cup canola oil
- 1 Tbsp. fresh lemon juice
- 3 garlic cloves
- ½ tsp. toasted sesame oil

  Salt

  Salad greens, roasted vegetables or grilled meats, for serving

In a blender, combine the tofu, sesame seeds, canola oil, lemon juice, garlic and sesame oil and puree until smooth. Season the dressing with salt and serve on salad greens or with roasted vegetables or grilled meats.

Seared Tofu Tabbouleh

Total **40 min**; Serves **4 to 6**

- 1¼ cups bulgur
- ⅓ cup extra-virgin olive oil

  One 14-oz. package firm tofu, drained and cubed
- 5 scallions, chopped, plus more for garnish
- 1 small tomato, chopped
- 1 Kirby cucumber, chopped
- 1 Tbsp. fresh lemon juice

  Salt and pepper

1. In a medium saucepan of boiling water, cook the bulgur until tender, about 12 minutes. Drain and return the bulgur to the pan. Cover and let stand for 10 minutes; fluff with a fork. Spread the bulgur on a baking sheet and let cool to room temperature.

2. In a large cast-iron skillet, heat 2 tablespoons of the oil. Cook the tofu and 5 chopped scallions over high heat, stirring, until golden and crisp in spots, about 5 minutes. Transfer to a large bowl. Stir in the bulgur, tomato, cucumber, lemon juice and the remaining oil and season with salt and pepper. Garnish with more chopped scallions and serve.

Crispy Tofu Steaks with Ginger Vinaigrette

Total **30 min**; Serves **4**

- 3 **Tbsp. minced peeled fresh ginger**
- 3 **Tbsp. minced scallion**
- 1 **Tbsp. distilled white vinegar**
- ⅔ **cup canola oil**

  Salt
- 1 **large egg**
- 1 **cup panko**

  One 14-oz. package firm tofu, drained and sliced 1 inch thick

1. In a small bowl, mix the ginger with the scallion, vinegar and ⅓ cup of the oil; season the vinaigrette with salt.

2. Beat the egg in a medium bowl. Spread the panko on a plate. Dip the tofu slices in the egg, then coat in the panko. In a large nonstick skillet, heat the remaining ⅓ cup of oil. Fry the tofu over moderate heat, turning, until golden and crispy, about 8 minutes. Season with salt and serve with the ginger vinaigrette.

Wine Vivid, yellow apple–scented Alsace Pinot Gris.

Tofu Masala

Total **30 min**; Serves **4**

3 Tbsp. canola oil

1 small onion, chopped

1 serrano chile, chopped

¼ cup finely chopped garlic

¼ cup finely chopped peeled
   fresh ginger

4 tsp. ground coriander

4 tsp. garam masala

2 medium tomatoes, chopped
   (4 cups)

   One 14-oz. package firm tofu,
   drained and cubed

   Chopped cilantro, for garnish

   Steamed basmati rice,
   for serving

In a large nonstick skillet, heat
the oil. Add the onion, serrano,
garlic, ginger, coriander, garam
masala and tomatoes and cook
over moderate heat, stirring,
until fragrant and saucy, about
8 minutes. Stir in the tofu and
1 cup of water and bring to a
simmer. Garnish with cilantro
and serve with basmati rice.

Wine Juicy, tropical fruit–
inflected South African
Chenin Blanc.

Summery Fresh Tomato Soup

Total **35 min**; Serves **4**

3 Tbsp. unsalted butter

¾ cup minced sweet onion,
  such as Vidalia

1½ lbs. tomatoes–peeled, seeded
  and chopped, with juices

1 tsp. tomato paste

2 cups low-sodium
  chicken broth

1 basil sprig

Salt and pepper

12 thin baguette slices, toasted

¼ cup plus 2 Tbsp. freshly grated
  Parmigiano-Reggiano cheese

1. In a large saucepan, melt the butter. Add the onion and cook over moderate heat, stirring, until softened, about 5 minutes. Add the tomatoes and their juices along with the tomato paste and cook, stirring, for 5 minutes. Add the broth and basil and season with salt and pepper. Simmer until the tomatoes are broken down, about 15 minutes. Discard the basil, transfer the soup to a blender or food processor and puree until smooth.

2. Preheat the broiler and arrange the baguette toasts on a baking sheet. Sprinkle with the cheese and broil just until melted, about 30 seconds. Serve the soup with the cheese toasts.

Make Ahead The soup can be refrigerated overnight.

Roasted Tomatoes with Anchovies and Capers

Active **30 min**; Total **4 hr**
Makes **about 3 cups**

2 large shallots, sliced
  ¼ inch thick

¼ cup extra-virgin olive oil,
  plus more for marinating

5 lbs. plum tomatoes–peeled,
  halved and seeded

Salt and pepper

One 2-oz. can anchovy fillets,
  drained and finely chopped

¼ cup drained capers

Grilled bread, for serving

1. Preheat the oven to 275°. In a large bowl, toss the shallots with 2 tablespoons of the olive oil and spread on a large, rimmed, parchment paper–lined baking sheet. In the same bowl, toss the tomatoes with the remaining 2 tablespoons of olive oil and season with salt and pepper. Arrange the tomatoes over the shallots, cut side up, and bake until the tomatoes are leathery but soft, about 3 hours. Let cool.

2. In a large jar or glass bowl, layer the tomatoes and shallots with the anchovies and capers. Cover with olive oil and let stand for 30 minutes or refrigerate overnight. Serve with grilled bread.

Make Ahead The roasted tomatoes can be refrigerated for up to 2 weeks; keep them covered with olive oil.

Pappardelle with Tomatoes, Almonds and Parmesan

Active **20 min**; Total **1 hr 30 min**
Serves **6**

1½ **lbs. heirloom tomatoes,
chopped into different sizes**

1 **Tbsp. red wine vinegar**

½ **cup extra-virgin olive oil**

2 **Tbsp. minced shallots**

1 **Tbsp. minced oregano**

¼ **cup shredded basil leaves**

1 **small fresh hot red chile,
minced**

Salt and pepper

1 **lb. pappardelle**

¼ **cup chopped marcona almonds**

¼ **cup freshly grated
Parmigiano-Reggiano cheese**

1. In a large bowl, combine the tomatoes with the vinegar, olive oil, shallots, oregano, basil and chile and season with salt and pepper. Let stand at room temperature for 1 hour.

2. In a large pot of salted boiling water, cook the pasta until al dente. Drain. Add the pasta to the tomatoes and toss. In a small bowl, mix the almonds and Parmigiano. Sprinkle over the pasta and serve right away.

Wine Red berry–scented, light-bodied red, like Beaujolais.

Tomato Salad with Horseradish Ranch Dressing

Total **20 min**; Serves **6**

- ¼ **cup mayonnaise**
- ¼ **cup buttermilk**
- 2 **Tbsp. prepared horseradish**
-    **Flaky sea salt and black pepper**
- 2½ **lbs. heirloom tomatoes and cherry tomatoes, chopped into different sizes**
- 2 **scallions, thinly sliced**

In a small bowl, whisk the mayonnaise with the buttermilk and horseradish and season with salt and pepper. Arrange the tomatoes on plates and top with the scallions. Drizzle with the dressing and serve right away.

Wine Crisp, tangy white, like Pinot Grigio.

Garlic-Toasted Tomato Tartines

Total **15 min**; Serves **6**

6 slices of Pullman bread

1 large garlic clove, halved

3 oz. French feta cheese, crumbled

¼ cup mayonnaise

2 Tbsp. minced chives

Flaky sea salt and pepper

2 lbs. mixed heirloom tomatoes and cherry tomatoes, cut into different sizes

Extra-virgin olive oil, for drizzling

Radish sprouts, for garnish

1. Light a grill or heat a grill pan. Grill the bread over moderately high heat until browned. Rub the toasts with the garlic halves.

2. In a medium bowl, mash the feta with the mayonnaise and chives and season with salt and pepper. Spread the feta mayonnaise on the garlic toasts and top with the tomatoes. Drizzle with olive oil and season with sea salt. Garnish with radish sprouts and serve right away.

Wine Juicy, watermelon- and strawberry-scented rosé.

BONUS RECIPE BY CHEF JACQUES PÉPIN

Garlicky Cherry Tomato and Bread Gratin

Active **20 min**; Total **1 hr**
Serves **6**

One 5-oz. piece of day-old French baguette with crust, cut into 1-inch cubes (5 cups)

1½ lbs. small cherry tomatoes

⅓ cup extra-virgin olive oil

3 medium garlic cloves, thinly sliced

½ cup chopped flat-leaf parsley

½ cup plus 2 Tbsp. freshly grated Parmigiano-Reggiano cheese

½ tsp. kosher salt

¼ tsp. freshly ground pepper

Preheat the oven to 375°. Lightly oil a 10-inch ceramic quiche dish. In a large bowl, toss the bread cubes with the tomatoes, olive oil, garlic, parsley, Parmigiano-Reggiano, salt and pepper. Scrape the mixture into the prepared dish and bake in the center of the oven for 35 minutes, or until the bread cubes are browned and crisp and the tomatoes are very tender. Serve warm or at room temperature.

Garlic-Toasted
Tomato Tartines

Turkey Tonnato

Turkey Curry Soup

Turkey–Stuffing Salad, p. 238

Turkey Reuben Hash, p. 238

Turkey Tonnato

Total **20 min**; Serves **4**

- 1 **lb. thinly sliced roast turkey breast**

  One 6½-oz. can tuna in water, drained
- ½ **cup canned chickpeas, rinsed**
- ¼ **cup yogurt**
- ½ **cup extra-virgin olive oil**
- ¼ **cup chopped drained capers**
- ½ **cup mixed chopped herbs, such as tarragon, chives and dill**

  Salt and pepper

Arrange the turkey slices on a platter. In a food processor, combine the tuna, chickpeas and yogurt. With the machine on, drizzle in the olive oil until the sauce is smooth. Transfer to a medium bowl, stir in the capers and herbs and season with salt and pepper. Spoon over the turkey and serve.

Wine Medium-bodied northern Italian white, like Arneis.

Turkey Curry Soup

Total **30 min**; Serves **4**

- 2 **Tbsp. canola oil**
- 2 **Tbsp. Thai red curry paste**
- ½ **small kabocha squash (1 lb.)– peeled, seeded and cut into 1½-inch pieces (4 cups)**
- 1 **cup unsweetened coconut milk**
- 1 **Tbsp. Asian fish sauce**
- ¾ **lb. roast turkey, shredded (3 cups)**
- 3 **Tbsp. fresh lime juice, plus lime wedges for serving**
- ½ **cup mixed chopped herbs, such as cilantro and basil**

  Salt and pepper

In a large saucepan, heat the oil. Add the curry paste and squash and cook over high heat, stirring, until lightly caramelized, 3 minutes. Add the coconut milk, fish sauce and 4 cups of water and bring to a boil. Cover and simmer until the squash is tender, about 15 minutes. Stir in the turkey, lime juice and herbs, season with salt and pepper and serve with lime wedges.

Turkey-Stuffing Salad

Total **30 min**; Serves **6**

- 1 Tbsp. Dijon mustard
- 1 Tbsp. fresh lemon juice
- ½ cup extra-virgin olive oil
- ¾ lb. roast turkey, chopped (3 cups)
- 3 celery ribs, thinly sliced
- 1 small fennel bulb, trimmed and very thinly sliced
- 1 Fuji or Honeycrisp apple, chopped
- 1 cup parsley leaves
- Salt and pepper
- Croutons, for garnish

In a large bowl, whisk the mustard with the lemon juice and olive oil. Add the turkey, celery, fennel, apple and parsley, season with salt and pepper and toss to coat. Transfer to a platter, top with croutons and serve.

Turkey Reuben Hash

Total **25 min**; Serves **4**

- 3 Tbsp. extra-virgin olive oil
- ½ small onion, finely chopped
- 1 baking potato, peeled and coarsely grated
- 1 cup drained sauerkraut (4 oz.)
- ½ lb. roast turkey, shredded (2 cups)
- 2 scallions, chopped
- ⅛ tsp. caraway seeds
- Salt and pepper

In a large cast-iron skillet, heat the olive oil. Add the onion and potato and cook over moderately high heat, stirring occasionally, until golden and tender, 7 to 8 minutes. Add the sauerkraut, turkey, scallions and caraway seeds and cook until golden, about 3 minutes. Season with salt and pepper and serve.

Turkey and Pinto Bean Chili

Active **20 min**; Total **1 hr 15 min**
Serves **6 to 8**

- ¼ cup extra-virgin olive oil
- 3 lbs. ground turkey
- 1 medium onion, cut into ½-inch dice
- 3 garlic cloves, minced
- 1½ Tbsp. chili powder
- 1 tsp. ground cumin
- 1 tsp. dried oregano
- ¾ tsp. chipotle powder
- 1 large carrot, cut into ¼-inch dice
- 1 red bell pepper, cut into ½-inch dice
- One 28-oz. can tomato puree
- Three 15-oz. cans pinto beans, drained
- ¾ cup lager
- 1 cup chicken stock or low-sodium broth
- 1 Tbsp. apple cider vinegar
- 1 tsp. chopped thyme leaves
- Salt and black pepper
- Chopped chives, for garnish

1. In a large Dutch oven, heat 1 tablespoon of the oil until shimmering. Add half of the turkey and cook over high heat, undisturbed, until browned on the bottom, about 3 minutes. Stir the turkey and cook until no pink remains, about 2 minutes longer. Transfer the cooked turkey to a bowl and repeat with 1 more tablespoon of oil and the remaining turkey.

2. Add the remaining 2 tablespoons of oil and the onion to the pot. Cook over moderate heat until softened, about 5 minutes. Add the garlic, chili powder, cumin, oregano and chipotle powder and cook, stirring, until fragrant, about 2 minutes. Return the turkey to the pot. Stir in the carrot, bell pepper, tomato puree, beans and lager and bring to a boil. Stir in the stock and vinegar, cover and simmer over low heat for 45 minutes. Add the thyme, season with salt and pepper and serve, garnished with chives.

Beer Crisp, malty lager.

Zucchini

242 **Zucchini Gratin**

242 **Zucchini Confetti Pasta with Dill and Walnuts**

245 **Grilled Zucchini and Lamb with Serrano Chile**

245 **Crispy Zucchini Pancakes**

Zucchini Gratin

Active **15 min**; Total **45 min**; Serves **6**

- 2 **Tbsp. extra-virgin olive oil, plus more for greasing**
- 4 **medium summer squash (zucchini and/or yellow squash), sliced lengthwise ⅛ inch thick**
- 3 **garlic cloves, sliced**

  Salt and pepper
- 1 **cup panko**
- 3 **oz. Gruyère cheese, shredded (1 cup)**

Preheat the oven to 450°. Grease a 2-quart baking dish. In a large bowl, combine the squash, garlic and 2 tablespoons of oil; season with salt and pepper and toss. Arrange the squash in the prepared dish and bake for 20 minutes, until tender. Sprinkle with the panko and cheese and bake for 10 minutes longer, until golden and crisp on top.

Zucchini Confetti Pasta with Dill and Walnuts

Total **25 min**; Serves **4**

- ½ **lb. spaghetti**
- 2 **Tbsp. extra-virgin olive oil**
- 3 **medium zucchini, grated on the large holes of a box grater and squeezed dry**
- 3 **anchovy fillets packed in oil, drained**
- 3 **garlic cloves, thinly sliced**
- 1 **Tbsp. fresh lemon juice**
- ½ **cup freshly grated Parmigiano-Reggiano cheese**

  Salt and pepper

  Chopped dill and chopped toasted walnuts, for garnish

1. In a large pot of salted boiling water, cook the spaghetti until al dente. Drain.

2. Meanwhile, in a large nonstick skillet, heat the olive oil. Add the zucchini, anchovies and garlic and cook over moderate heat, stirring, until the zucchini is tender and the anchovies have dissolved, about 5 minutes. Stir in the spaghetti, lemon juice and cheese and season with salt and pepper. Serve, garnished with chopped dill and chopped toasted walnuts.

Wine Citrusy Chilean Sauvignon Blanc.

Grilled Zucchini and Lamb
with Serrano Chile

Grilled Zucchini and Lamb with Serrano Chile

Active **20 min**; Total **35 min**; Serves **4**

- 1 lb. trimmed lamb shoulder, cut into 1½-inch pieces
- 2 small summer squash (zucchini and/or yellow squash), cut into 2-inch pieces
- 2 Tbsp. Asian fish sauce
- 2 Tbsp. distilled white vinegar
- ¼ cup canola oil

  Thinly sliced serrano chile and chopped cilantro, for garnish

  Lime wedges, for serving

Light a grill. In a large bowl, toss the lamb and squash with the fish sauce, vinegar and oil. Let stand for 15 minutes. Grill the lamb and squash over moderate heat, turning, until the lamb is medium within, about 10 minutes. Transfer to plates. Garnish with chile and cilantro and serve with lime wedges.

Wine Peach-inflected, full-bodied Rhône white.

Crispy Zucchini Pancakes

Total **25 min**; Makes **6 pancakes**

- 2 medium summer squash (zucchini and/or yellow squash), grated on the medium holes of a box grater and squeezed dry
- 2 scallions, thinly sliced
- 1 jalapeño, thinly sliced
- 1 large egg, beaten
- ½ cup all-purpose flour
- 2 tsp. baking powder

  Salt and pepper
- 6 Tbsp. canola oil

  Lemon wedges and sour cream, for serving

1. In a medium bowl, combine the squash with the scallions, jalapeño, egg, flour and baking powder and season with salt and pepper. Mix gently just to combine.

2. In a large nonstick skillet, heat 2 tablespoons of the oil. Spoon 3 heaping ⅓-cup mounds of the batter into the skillet and press lightly to flatten them. Cook over moderate heat until golden, about 3 minutes. Flip the pancakes, add 1 tablespoon of the oil and cook until golden and crisp, 2 minutes longer. Drain on paper towels. Repeat with the remaining oil and batter. Serve the pancakes hot, with lemon wedges and sour cream.

Wine Fruit-forward sparkling wine, like Prosecco.

Fresh Grape Soda,
p. 116

Contributors

Recipes

Justin Chapple
Apricots, pp. 16–19
Beef, pp. 34–36
Canned Tuna, pp. 64–66
Cauliflower, pp. 73, 74
Chicken, pp. 81, 82
Chickpeas, pp. 84–87
Green Beans, pp. 118–121
Lamb, pp. 144–147
Pasta, pp. 166–169
Pork, pp. 174–177
Salmon, pp. 197, 198
Shrimp, pp. 204–206

Kay Chun
Asparagus, pp. 20–23
Avocado, pp. 24–27
Beets, pp. 38–40
Brussels Sprouts, pp. 50–53
Cabbage, pp. 61, 62
Carrots, pp. 69–71
Cherries, pp. 76–78
Corn, pp. 88–91
Cucumbers, pp. 92–94
Eggplant, pp. 99, 100
Eggs, pp. 102–105
Fish Fillets and Steaks,
    pp. 108–111
Ham, pp. 129, 130
Kale, pp. 139, 140
Lentils, pp. 148–150
Mushrooms, pp. 155–157
Peppers, pp. 171, 172
Potatoes, pp. 179–181
Quinoa, pp. 185–187
Rice, pp. 191, 192
Sausage, pp. 200–203
Snap Peas, pp. 208–211
Spinach, pp. 213, 214
Sweet Potatoes, pp. 220–223
Tofu, pp. 227–229
Turkey, pp. 237, 238
Zucchini, pp. 242–245

Ben Mims
Bananas, pp. 30–33
Blueberries, pp. 42–45
Grapes, pp. 114–117
Ground Beef, pp. 123–125
Hot Peppers, pp. 132–135
Oranges, pp. 160–163
Strawberries, pp. 216–219

Grace Parisi
Apples, pp. 13–15
Broccoli, pp. 46–49
Butternut Squash, pp. 54–57
Tomatoes, pp. 230–234

Photographs

Chris Court pp. 47, 49, 221, 223

Nicole Franzen pp. 16, 17, 18, 19, 208, 209, 210

Christina Holmes pp. 12, 15, 24, 25, 26, 54, 55, 57, 80, 128, 138, 178, 190, 236

John Kernick pp. 50, 51, 52, 68, 71, 76, 77, 79, 89, 90, 92, 95

Line Klein p. 60

Eva Kolenko pp. 8, 10–11, 28–29, 30, 31, 32, 33, 34, 35, 37, 42, 43, 44, 45, 58–59, 64, 65, 67, 72, 75, 84, 85, 86, 87, 96–97, 102, 103, 104, 105, 106–107, 108, 109, 111, 112–113, 114, 115, 116, 117, 118, 119, 120, 121, 122, 124, 125, 126–127, 132, 133, 134, 136–137, 142–143, 144, 145, 146, 147, 149, 151, 152–153, 154, 156, 157, 158–159, 161, 162, 163, 164–165, 174, 175, 176, 182–183, 184, 186, 187, 188–189, 194–195, 196, 199, 200, 201, 202, 203, 212, 216, 217, 218, 224–225, 226, 228, 229, 240–241, 243, 244, 246

Jonathan Lovekin p. 98

Johnny Miller pp. 21, 23, 24, 25

Con Poulos pp. 170, 205, 231, 232, 233, 235

Andrew Purcell pp. 166, 167, 168, 169

Fredrika Stjärne pp. 38, 41

Index

A

ANCHOVIES

Broccoli-Anchovy Fettuccine, 48

Garlicky Kale-and-Provolone Grinders, 140

Grilled Marinated Cucumbers and Eggplant with Basil, 94

Potted Ham with Cabbage and Pickles, 62

Roasted Asparagus with Lemony Breadcrumbs, 23

Roasted Tomatoes with Anchovies and Capers, 230

Warm Escarole Salad with Sausage Vinaigrette, 203

Zucchini Confetti Pasta with Dill and Walnuts, 242

APPLES

Apple Sandwiches, 13

Apples on Horseback, 14

Butternut Squash, Apple and Chicken Pan Roast, 55

Caramel-Apple Ice Cream, 14

Grilled Rib Eye Steaks with Apple-Radish Vinaigrette, 36

Hard Cider Sangria, 15

Potato-Apple-Dill Pancakes, 180

Salmon Sandwiches with Bacon and Apple-Horseradish Mayo, 198

Sausage and Apple Frittata with Dill, 105

Savory Apple Compote, 13

Thai Brussels Sprout Salad, 50

Turkey-Stuffing Salad, 238

APRICOTS

Apricot and Ricotta Tartines, 17

Apricot-Glazed Butternut Squash Tart, 57

Charred Green Beans with Apricots, 16

Honey-Thyme Chicken and Apricot Kebabs, 18

Lemony Apricot Clafoutis, 19

ARTICHOKES

Lemony Tuna and Artichoke Dip, 66

ASPARAGUS

Asparagus Pickles, 20

Asparagus Tabbouleh, 20

Asparagus Vinaigrette, 22

Pasta with Asparagus Pesto, 22

Roasted Asparagus with Lemony Breadcrumbs, 23

AVOCADOS

Avocado-Hummus Dip, 25

Avocado Tartare, 24

Cumin Oil–Fried Egg and Avocado Toasts, 104

Grilled Eggplant Tortas, 100

Pink Grapefruit and Avocado Salad, 27

Roasted Carrot and Avocado Salad, 27

Salmon and Citrus Salad with Poppy Seed Dressing, 197

Spinach Salad with Walnut Vinaigrette, 214

B

BACON

Adobo Meat Loaves, 123

Apple Cider–Braised Cabbage, 63

Eggplant Potato Salad, 100

Ham, Escarole and White Bean Stew, 131

Salmon Sandwiches with Bacon and Apple-Horseradish Mayo, 198

Swordfish Spiedini, 110

BANANAS

Banana-Nut Truffles, 32

Banana Snacking Cake, 33

Banana-Strawberry Tartines, 30

Spiced Rice Breakfast Porridge, 192

Tropical Banana Roast, 31

BASIL

Chicken-Cabbage Salad, 62

Double-Pea Sauté with Ground Pork, 208

Eggplant Noodle Salad, 99

Grilled Marinated Cucumbers and Eggplant with Basil, 94

Kale Rice Bowl, 139

Penne with Chicken and Pickled Peppers, 168

Raw Beet and Kalamata Olive Relish, 39

Sweet Potatoes with Almond Pesto, 122

Thai Brussels Sprout Salad, 50

BEANS. See also CHICKPEAS; GREEN BEANS; LENTILS

Ham, Escarole and White Bean Stew, 131

Turkey and Pinto Bean Chili, 239

Tuscan White Bean and Escarole Soup with Tuna, 65

BEEF

Adobo Meat Loaves, 123

Beet and Beef Burgers, 125

Bulgogi-Style Pepper Steak Sandwiches, 172

Coconut Curried Beef Noodles, 124

Grilled Rib Eye Steaks with Apple-Radish Vinaigrette, 36

Skirt Steak Quinoa Bowls with Ginger-Sesame Dressing, 185

Spring Beef Stew, 35

Steak Tacos with Pineapple, 34

Sweet-and-Spicy Grilled Beef Short Ribs, 36

Yorkshire Pudding Bake with Beef and Cheddar, 123

BEETS

Beet and Beef Burgers, 125

Beet and Lentil Salad with Beet Greens, 40

Beet and Potato Latkes, 40

Crunchy Carrot and Beet Salad with Herbs, 70

Pickled Beets and Eggs, 38

Raw Beet and Kalamata Olive Relish, 39

Salt-Baked Caraway Beets, 39

BLACKBERRIES

Blackberry-Glazed Pork Chops with Broccolini, 177

BLUEBERRIES

Blueberry Cheesecake Mousse, 43

Blueberry Dutch Baby, 42

Blueberry Vinaigrette, 44

Maraschino Blueberries, 45

BREADS. See also CROSTINI AND TOASTS

Caramelized Panzanella with Strawberries, 216

Carrot, Coconut and Zucchini Bread, 70

Chicken Roasted on Bread with
Caperberries and Charred
Lemons, 82
Garlicky Cherry Tomato and Bread
Gratin, 234
Sausage and Cheddar Muffins, 200
Spinach Spoon Bread, 215

BROCCOLI
Broccoli-Anchovy Fettuccine, 48
Broccoli Cheese Dunk, 48
Creamy Roasted Broccoli Soup, 46
Flash-Roasted Broccoli with Spicy
Crumbs, 46
Warm Kale and Broccoli Stem
Salad with Leek Vinaigrette, 49

BROCCOLINI
Blackberry-Glazed Pork Chops
with Broccolini, 177
Salmon, Broccolini and Fresh Red
Chile Papillotes, 197

BRUSSELS SPROUTS
Brussels Sprout Frittata, 51
Cabbage Slaw, 61
Spaghetti with Brussels Sprout and
Sausage Breadcrumbs, 53
Thai Brussels Sprout Salad, 50
Whole Roast Chicken with
40 Brussels Sprouts, 53

BUTTERNUT SQUASH
Apricot-Glazed Butternut Squash
Tart, 57
Butternut Squash, Apple and
Chicken Pan Roast, 55
Chipotle-Butternut Squash Soup
with Chive Cream, 54
Mashed Butternut Squash with
Roasted Garlic, 56
Squash Rösti Cakes with Sour
Cream and Salmon Caviar, 56

C

CABBAGE
Apple Cider–Braised Cabbage, 63
Cabbage Slaw, 61
Chicken-Cabbage Salad, 62
Fish Soup with Cabbage and
Potatoes, 111
Fresh Cabbage Kimchi, 61

Gingery Creamed Kale and
Cabbage, 141
Potted Ham with Cabbage and
Pickles, 62

CAKES
Banana Snacking Cake, 33
Roasted Grape Cake, 115
Strawberry Shortcake, 218

CAPERS
Beet and Beef Burgers, 125
Egg Salad with Herbs and
Pickles, 103
Herb-Marinated Peppers and
Tuna, 171
Roasted Tomatoes with Anchovies
and Capers, 230
Sea Bass Dill Meunière, 109
Turkey Tonnato, 237
Warm Escarole Salad with Sausage
Vinaigrette, 203

CARROTS
Carrot, Coconut and Zucchini
Bread, 70
Carrot-Pear Shrub, 71
Chicken-Cabbage Salad, 62
Crunchy Carrot and Beet Salad
with Herbs, 70
Curry-Roasted Carrots with Carrot
Top Gremolata, 69
Nutty Carrot Pilaf, 69
Spring Beef Stew, 35
Roasted Carrot and Avocado
Salad, 27
Warm Lentil and Carrot Salad with
Feta Dressing, 148

CAULIFLOWER
Cauliflower Puree with
Horseradish and Caraway, 73
Faux Tso's Cauliflower, 74
Silky Cauliflower Soup with
Charmoula and Almonds, 73
Stir-Fried Cauliflower "Rice," 74

CHEESE. See also PARMESAN
Apples on Horseback, 14
Apricot and Ricotta Tartines, 17
Baked Rigatoni with Eggplant,
Tomatoes and Ricotta, 101
Broccoli Cheese Dunk, 48
Cacio e Pepe Pasta Pie, 167
Crispy Baked Jalapeño Poppers, 132

Fettuccine with Shrimp, 166
Garlicky Kale-and-Provolone
Grinders, 140
Garlic-Toasted Tomato
Tartines, 234
Grape and Walnut Crostini with
Roquefort, 114
Mexican Eggs Baked in Tomato
Sauce, 102
Muffuletta Calzone, 129
Mushroom Poutine, 157
Open-Face Monte Cristos, 130
Quinoa-Dill Omelet with Feta, 186
Sausage and Apple Frittata with
Dill, 105
Sausage and Cheddar Muffins, 200
Sausage and Fennel Parm
Heroes, 202
Spanish-Style Chickpea
Quesadillas, 87
Warm Lentil and Carrot Salad with
Feta Dressing, 148
Yorkshire Pudding Bake with Beef
and Cheddar, 123
Zucchini Gratin, 242

CHERRIES
Cherry Hand Pies, 77
Cherry-Lime Buttermilk Pudding
Cups, 78
Israeli Couscous with Cherries and
Olives, 76
Pork and Sausage Meat Loaf with
Cherries, 78

CHICKEN
Butternut Squash, Apple and
Chicken Pan Roast, 55
Chicken and Pepper Cacciatore, 173
Chicken-Cabbage Salad, 62
Chicken Caesar Skewers, 81
Chicken-Chile Soup, 82
Chicken Roasted on Bread with
Caperberries and Charred
Lemons, 82
Chile-Chicken Saltimbocca, 133
Coconut Rice Salad, 191
Honey Mustard Chicken, 83
Honey-Orange Chicken, 160
Honey-Thyme Chicken and
Apricot Kebabs, 18

Lemon-Shallot-Marinated
Chicken, 83

Lentil and Chicken Cassoulet, 150

Penne with Chicken and Pickled
Peppers, 168

Sesame-Ginger Chicken
Meatballs, 81

Whole Roast Chicken with
40 Brussels Sprouts, 53

CHICKPEAS

Avocado-Hummus Dip, 25

Chickpea and Swiss Chard Chili, 85

Chickpea Salad Sandwiches, 84

Indian Fried Rice with Chickpeas
and Spinach, 192

Kale Caesar with Fried
Chickpeas, 86

Orecchiette with Sausage,
Chickpeas and Mint, 169

Snap Pea Falafel Salad, 211

Spanish-Style Chickpea
Quesadillas, 87

Turkey Tonnato, 237

CHILES. *See also* **PEPPERS**

Asparagus Pickles, 20

Charred Green Beans with
Apricots, 16

Chicken-Cabbage Salad, 62

Chicken-Chile Soup, 82

Chile-Chicken Saltimbocca, 133

Chile-Cilantro Pesto, 135

Crispy Baked Jalapeño Poppers, 132

Crispy Zucchini Pancakes, 245

Curry-Roasted Carrots with Carrot
Top Gremolata, 69

Grape Salsa Verde, 117

Green Bean and Scallion
Pancake, 119

Grilled Zucchini and Lamb with
Serrano Chile, 245

Mashed Butternut Squash with
Roasted Garlic, 56

Mexican Eggs Baked in Tomato
Sauce, 102

Salmon, Broccolini and Fresh Red
Chile Papillotes, 197

Scallops with Thai Chile Sauce, 134

Serrano Chile and Potato Hash, 135

Sichuan-Style Green Beans with
Pork, 120

Spicy Fideos with Pork, 174

Spicy Pickled Peppers, 172

Thai Brussels Sprout Salad, 50

Tuna Banh Mi, 64

CHOCOLATE

Banana-Nut Truffles, 32

CILANTRO

Chicken-Cabbage Salad, 62

Chile-Cilantro Pesto, 135

Curry-Roasted Carrots with Carrot
Top Gremolata, 69

Grape Salsa Verde, 117

Kale Rice Bowl, 139

Shrimp Salad with Green Curry
Dressing, 204

Thai Brussels Sprout Salad, 50

COCONUT AND COCONUT MILK

Carrot, Coconut and Zucchini
Bread, 70

Coconut Curried Beef Noodles, 124

Coconut Lamb Curry with Sweet
Potatoes, 144

Coconut Rice Salad, 191

Thai Glazed Corn, 91

Tropical Banana Roast, 31

Turkey Curry Soup, 237

CORN

Corn-Shrimp Dumplings, 88

Parmesan Corn Butter, 91

Skillet Corn with Bulgur, 88

Thai Glazed Corn, 91

CROSTINI AND TOASTS

Apricot and Ricotta Tartines, 17

Banana-Strawberry Tartines, 30

Cumin Oil–Fried Egg and Avocado
Toasts, 104

Garlic-Toasted Tomato
Tartines, 234

Grape and Walnut Crostini with
Roquefort, 114

CUCUMBERS

Cucumber and Salami Fried Rice
with Arugula, 93

Cucumber and Sugar Snap Salad
with Nutty Granola, 93

Cucumber Gazpacho with
Shrimp, 92

Dill Pickles, 94

Grilled Marinated Cucumbers and
Eggplant with Basil, 94

Spiced Lamb Sliders with Harissa
Mayonnaise and Cucumber, 147

D

DESSERTS

Apricot-Glazed Butternut Squash
Tart, 57

Balsamic Strawberries with
Strawberry Sorbet, 219

Banana-Nut Truffles, 32

Banana Snacking Cake, 33

Banana-Strawberry Tartines, 30

Blueberry Cheesecake Mousse, 43

Blueberry Dutch Baby, 42

Caramel-Apple Ice Cream, 14

Caramelized Panzanella with
Strawberries, 216

Carrot, Coconut and Zucchini
Bread, 70

Cherry Hand Pies, 77

Cherry-Lime Buttermilk Pudding
Cups, 78

Fresh Strawberry Sauce, 219

Lemony Apricot Clafoutis, 19

Maraschino Blueberries, 45

Orange-Almond Parfaits, 163

Orange Caramel Sauce, 162

Rice Pudding Brûlée, 193

Roasted Grape Cake, 115

Strawberry-Prosecco Gelées, 217

Strawberry Shortcake, 218

Tropical Banana Roast, 31

DILL

Dill Pickles, 94

Potato-Apple-Dill Pancakes, 180

Quinoa-Dill Omelet with Feta, 186

Sausage and Apple Frittata with
Dill, 105

Sea Bass Dill Meunière, 109

Zucchini Confetti Pasta with Dill
and Walnuts, 242

DRINKS

Carrot-Pear Shrub, 71

Fresh Grape Soda, 116

Hard Cider Sangria, 15

E

EGGPLANT

Baked Rigatoni with Eggplant, Tomatoes and Ricotta, 101
Eggplant Noodle Salad, 99
Eggplant Potato Salad, 100
Grilled Eggplant Tortas, 100
Grilled Marinated Cucumbers and Eggplant with Basil, 94
Pork and Eggplant Stir-Fry, 99

EGGS

Brussels Sprout Frittata, 51
Cumin Oil–Fried Egg and Avocado Toasts, 104
Egg Salad with Herbs and Pickles, 103
Mexican Eggs Baked in Tomato Sauce, 102
Pickled Beets and Eggs, 38
Quinoa-Dill Omelet with Feta, 186
Sausage and Apple Frittata with Dill, 105
Tortilla Española, 181

F

FENNEL

Fennel-Rubbed Pork Tenderloin with Fingerling Potatoes and Lemon, 175
Sausage and Fennel Parm Heroes, 202
Turkey-Stuffing Salad, 238

FISH. *See also* **ANCHOVIES; SALMON; TUNA**

Fish Soup with Cabbage and Potatoes, 111
Grilled Halibut Dip, 110
Sea Bass Dill Meunière, 109
Smoky Fishwiches, 108
Swordfish Spiedini, 110

G

GARLIC

Creamy Sesame-Garlic Tofu Dressing, 227
Garlicky Cherry Tomato and Bread Gratin, 234
Garlicky Kale-and-Provolone Grinders, 140

Garlicky Mushroom Pasta with Parsley, 155
Garlic-Toasted Tomato Tartines, 234
Herb-Marinated Peppers and Tuna, 171
Mashed Butternut Squash with Roasted Garlic, 56

GINGER

Carrot-Pear Shrub, 71
Crispy Tofu Steaks with Ginger Vinaigrette, 228
Fresh Grape Soda, 116
Gingery Creamed Kale and Cabbage, 141
Skirt Steak Quinoa Bowls with Ginger-Sesame Dressing, 185

GRAINS. *See also* **QUINOA; RICE**

Asparagus Tabbouleh, 20
Seared Tofu Tabbouleh, 227
Skillet Corn with Bulgur, 88
Snap Pea Falafel Salad, 211
Warm Mushroom-Barley Salad, 156

GRAPEFRUIT

Cabbage Slaw, 61
Pink Grapefruit and Avocado Salad, 27
Salmon and Citrus Salad with Poppy Seed Dressing, 197

GRAPES

Fresh Grape Soda, 116
Grape and Walnut Crostini with Roquefort, 114
Grape Salsa Verde, 117
Roasted Grape Cake, 115

GREEN BEANS

Bloody Mary–Pickled Green Beans, 118
Charred Green Beans with Apricots, 16
Green Bean and Scallion Pancake, 119
Sichuan-Style Green Beans with Pork, 120
Tempura Green Beans with Old Bay and Lemon, 121
Warm Potato and Green Bean Salad, 179

GREENS. *See also* **KALE; LETTUCE**

Beet and Lentil Salad with Beet Greens, 40
Chickpea and Swiss Chard Chili, 85
Cucumber and Salami Fried Rice with Arugula, 93
Ham, Escarole and White Bean Stew, 131
Quinoa Pilaf with Dates, Olives and Arugula, 185
Tuscan White Bean and Escarole Soup with Tuna, 65
Warm Escarole Salad with Sausage Vinaigrette, 203

H

HAM

Country Ham Flapjacks with Maple Syrup, 130
Ham, Escarole and White Bean Stew, 131
Muffuletta Calzone, 129
Open-Face Monte Cristos, 130
Potted Ham with Cabbage and Pickles, 62
Spring Ham Steaks with Sweet Pea–Leek Pan Sauce, 129
Warm Snap Peas with Ham and Tarragon Butter, 209

HERBS. *See also specific herbs*

Chipotle–Butternut Squash Soup with Chive Cream, 54
Crunchy Carrot and Beet Salad with Herbs, 70
Egg Salad with Herbs and Pickles, 103
Honey-Thyme Chicken and Apricot Kebabs, 18
Israeli Couscous with Cherries and Olives, 76
Mushroom Carpaccio with Chive Oil, 155
Salmon and Cherry Tomato Skewers with Rosemary Vinaigrette, 198
Warm Snap Peas with Ham and Tarragon Butter, 209

K

KALE

Cacio e Pepe–Style Braised Kale, 140

Garlicky Kale-and-Provolone Grinders, 140

Gingery Creamed Kale and Cabbage, 141

Kale Caesar with Fried Chickpeas, 86

Kale Rice Bowl, 139

Nutty Baby Kale Chips, 139

Warm Kale and Broccoli Stem Salad with Leek Vinaigrette, 49

L

LAMB

Coconut Lamb Curry with Sweet Potatoes, 144

Grilled Lamb Loin Chops with Pomegranate Relish, 146

Grilled Zucchini and Lamb with Serrano Chile, 245

Simplest Lamb Bolognese with Pappardelle, 145

Spiced Lamb Sliders with Harissa Mayonnaise and Cucumber, 147

LEMONS AND LEMON JUICE

Chicken Roasted on Bread with Caperberries and Charred Lemons, 82

Fennel-Rubbed Pork Tenderloin with Fingerling Potatoes and Lemon, 175

Lemon-Shallot-Marinated Chicken, 83

Lemony Apricot Clafoutis, 19

Lemony Tuna and Artichoke Dip, 66

Roasted Asparagus with Lemony Breadcrumbs, 23

Tempura Green Beans with Old Bay and Lemon, 121

LENTILS

Beet and Lentil Salad with Beet Greens, 40

Fried Spiced Red Lentils, 150

Lentil and Chicken Cassoulet, 150

Warm Lentil and Carrot Salad with Feta Dressing, 148

Yellow Lentil Dal with Tofu, 148

LETTUCE

Shrimp Salad with Green Curry Dressing, 204

Skirt Steak Quinoa Bowls with Ginger-Sesame Dressing, 185

LIMES AND LIME JUICE

Carrot-Pear Shrub, 71

Cherry-Lime Buttermilk Pudding Cups, 78

Chicken-Cabbage Salad, 62

Fresh Grape Soda, 116

Grape Salsa Verde, 117

Shrimp Salad with Green Curry Dressing, 204

Thai Brussels Sprout Salad, 50

Tropical Banana Roast, 31

M

MINT

Asparagus Tabbouleh, 20

Charred Green Beans with Apricots, 16

Grilled Lamb Loin Chops with Pomegranate Relish, 146

Orecchiette with Sausage, Chickpeas and Mint, 169

Shrimp Salad with Green Curry Dressing, 204

MUSHROOMS

Garlicky Mushroom Pasta with Parsley, 155

Mushroom Carpaccio with Chive Oil, 155

Mushroom Poutine, 157

Spinach Salad with Walnut Vinaigrette, 214

Sweet Potato and Mushroom Salad, 222

Warm Mushroom-Barley Salad, 156

N

NOODLES

Asian Pork Noodles with Spinach, 214

Chicken-Cabbage Salad, 62

Coconut Curried Beef Noodles, 124

Eggplant Noodle Salad, 99

NUTS

Apricot-Glazed Butternut Squash Tart, 57

Banana-Nut Truffles, 32

Grape and Walnut Crostini with Roquefort, 114

Nutty Baby Kale Chips, 139

Nutty Carrot Pilaf, 69

Orange-Almond Parfaits, 163

Pappardelle with Tomatoes, Almonds and Parmesan, 232

Quinoa with Spinach and Roasted Almonds, 213

Roasted Carrot and Avocado Salad, 27

Spinach Salad with Walnut Vinaigrette, 214

Sweet Potatoes with Almond Pesto, 222

Warm Kale and Broccoli Stem Salad with Leek Vinaigrette, 49

Zucchini Confetti Pasta with Dill and Walnuts, 242

O

OATS

Spiced Rice Breakfast Porridge, 192

OLIVES

Cabbage Slaw, 61

Israeli Couscous with Cherries and Olives, 76

Muffuletta Calzone, 129

Quinoa Pilaf with Dates, Olives and Arugula, 185

Raw Beet and Kalamata Olive Relish, 39

ONIONS

Grape Salsa Verde, 117

Spinach and Caramelized Onion Dip, 213

Tortilla Española, 181

ORANGES AND ORANGE JUICE

Cabbage Slaw, 61

Honey-Orange Chicken, 160

Orange-Almond Parfaits, 163

Orange Caramel Sauce, 162

Roasted Orange Marmalade, 160

Salmon and Citrus Salad with Poppy Seed Dressing, 197

P

PARMESAN
Baked Rigatoni with Eggplant, Tomatoes and Ricotta, 101
Baked Shrimp Risotto, 191
Broccoli-Anchovy Fettuccine, 48
Cacio e Pepe Pasta Pie, 167
Cacio e Pepe–Style Braised Kale, 140
Garlicky Cherry Tomato and Bread Gratin, 234
Kale Caesar with Fried Chickpeas, 86
Lemony Tuna and Artichoke Dip, 66
Pappardelle with Tomatoes, Almonds and Parmesan, 232
Parmesan Corn Butter, 91

PARSLEY
Asparagus Tabbouleh, 20
Broccoli-Anchovy Fettuccine, 48
Chile-Cilantro Pesto, 135
Egg Salad with Herbs and Pickles, 103
Garlicky Cherry Tomato and Bread Gratin, 234
Garlicky Mushroom Pasta with Parsley, 155
Raw Beet and Kalamata Olive Relish, 39
Roasted Carrot and Avocado Salad, 27
Turkey-Stuffing Salad, 238

PASTA. *See also* **NOODLES**
Angry Shrimp Spaghettini, 206
Baked Rigatoni with Eggplant, Tomatoes and Ricotta, 101
Broccoli-Anchovy Fettuccine, 48
Cacio e Pepe Pasta Pie, 167
Fettuccine with Shrimp, 166
Garlicky Mushroom Pasta with Parsley, 155
Israeli Couscous with Cherries and Olives, 76
Mixed Bell Pepper Pasta, 171
Orecchiette with Sausage, Chickpeas and Mint, 169
Pappardelle with Tomatoes, Almonds and Parmesan, 232

Pasta with Asparagus Pesto, 22
Penne with Chicken and Pickled Peppers, 168
Simplest Lamb Bolognese with Pappardelle, 145
Spaghetti with Brussels Sprout and Sausage Breadcrumbs, 53
Spicy Fideos with Pork, 174
Zucchini Confetti Pasta with Dill and Walnuts, 242

PEARS
Carrot-Pear Shrub, 71

PEAS
Cucumber and Sugar Snap Salad with Nutty Granola, 93
Double-Pea Sauté with Ground Pork, 208
Snap Pea and Radish Salad with Tahini Dressing, 211
Snap Pea Falafel Salad, 211
Spring Beef Stew, 35
Spring Ham Steaks with Sweet Pea–Leek Pan Sauce, 129
Warm Snap Peas with Ham and Tarragon Butter, 209

PEPPERS. *See also* **CHILES**
Broccoli-Anchovy Fettuccine, 48
Bulgogi-Style Pepper Steak Sandwiches, 172
Chicken and Pepper Cacciatore, 173
Herb-Marinated Peppers and Tuna, 171
Mixed Bell Pepper Pasta, 171
Muffuletta Calzone, 129
Penne with Chicken and Pickled Peppers, 168
Spicy Pickled Peppers, 172

PICKLES
Asparagus Pickles, 20
Bloody Mary–Pickled Green Beans, 118
Dill Pickles, 94
Egg Salad with Herbs and Pickles, 103
Penne with Chicken and Pickled Peppers, 168
Pickled Beets and Eggs, 38
Potted Ham with Cabbage and Pickles, 62
Spicy Pickled Peppers, 172

PORK
Asian Pork Noodles with Spinach, 214
Blackberry-Glazed Pork Chops with Broccolini, 177
Double-Pea Sauté with Ground Pork, 208
Fennel-Rubbed Pork Tenderloin with Fingerling Potatoes and Lemon, 175
Kale Rice Bowl, 139
Orecchiette with Sausage, Chickpeas and Mint, 169
Pork and Eggplant Stir-Fry, 99
Pork and Sausage Meat Loaf with Cherries, 78
Quinoa-Pork Meatballs, 187
Sichuan-Style Green Beans with Pork, 120
Spaghetti with Brussels Sprout and Sausage Breadcrumbs, 53
Spicy Fideos with Pork, 174
Vietnamese Pork Burgers, 177

POTATOES. *See also* **SWEET POTATOES**
Accordion Potatoes, 180
Beet and Potato Latkes, 40
Boiled Potatoes with Sage Butter, 181
Brussels Sprout Frittata, 51
Crispy Buffalo-Style Potatoes, 179
Eggplant Potato Salad, 100
Fennel-Rubbed Pork Tenderloin with Fingerling Potatoes and Lemon, 175
Fish Soup with Cabbage and Potatoes, 111
Potato-Apple-Dill Pancakes, 180
Sausage Choucroute, 201
Serrano Chile and Potato Hash, 135
Squash Rösti Cakes with Sour Cream and Caviar, 56
Tortilla Española, 181
Turkey Reuben Hash, 238
Warm Potato and Green Bean Salad, 179

PUMPKIN SEEDS
Nutty Carrot Pilaf, 69

Q

QUINOA
Quinoa-Dill Omelet with Feta, 186
Quinoa Pilaf with Dates, Olives and Arugula, 185
Quinoa-Pork Meatballs, 187
Quinoa with Spinach and Roasted Almonds, 213
Skirt Steak Quinoa Bowls with Ginger-Sesame Dressing, 185

R

RADISHES
Grilled Rib Eye Steaks with Apple-Radish Vinaigrette, 36
Quinoa with Spinach and Roasted Almonds, 213
Snap Pea and Radish Salad with Tahini Dressing, 211

RICE
Baked Shrimp Risotto, 191
Coconut Rice Salad, 191
Indian Fried Rice with Chickpeas and Spinach, 192
Kale Rice Bowl, 139
Nutty Carrot Pilaf, 69
Rice Pudding Brûlée, 193
Spiced Rice Breakfast Porridge, 192

S

SAGE
Boiled Potatoes with Sage Butter, 181
Butternut Squash, Apple and Chicken Pan Roast, 55
Salt-Baked Caraway Beets, 39
Yorkshire Pudding Bake with Beef and Cheddar, 123

SALADS
Beet and Lentil Salad with Beet Greens, 40
Chicken-Cabbage Salad, 62
Coconut Rice Salad, 191
Crunchy Carrot and Beet Salad with Herbs, 70
Cucumber and Sugar Snap Salad with Nutty Granola, 93
Eggplant Potato Salad, 100

Kale Caesar with Fried Chickpeas, 86
Pink Grapefruit and Avocado Salad, 27
Roasted Carrot and Avocado Salad, 27
Salmon and Citrus Salad with Poppy Seed Dressing, 197
Shrimp Salad with Green Curry Dressing, 204
Snap Pea and Radish Salad with Tahini Dressing, 211
Snap Pea Falafel Salad, 211
Spinach Salad with Walnut Vinaigrette, 214
Sweet Potato and Mushroom Salad, 222
Thai Brussels Sprout Salad, 50
Tomato Salad with Horseradish Ranch Dressing, 233
Turkey-Stuffing Salad, 238
Warm Escarole Salad with Sausage Vinaigrette, 203
Warm Kale and Broccoli Stem Salad with Leek Vinaigrette, 49
Warm Lentil and Carrot Salad with Feta Dressing, 148
Warm Mushroom-Barley Salad, 156
Warm Potato and Green Bean Salad, 179

SALMON
Salmon and Cherry Tomato Skewers with Rosemary Vinaigrette, 198
Salmon and Citrus Salad with Poppy Seed Dressing, 197
Salmon, Broccolini and Fresh Red Chile Papillotes, 197
Salmon Sandwiches with Bacon and Apple-Horseradish Mayo, 198

SANDWICHES
Bulgogi-Style Pepper Steak Sandwiches, 172
Chickpea Salad Sandwiches, 84
Garlicky Kale-and-Provolone Grinders, 140
Grilled Eggplant Tortas, 100
Muffuletta Calzone, 129

Open-Face Monte Cristos, 130
Salmon Sandwiches with Bacon and Apple-Horseradish Mayo, 198
Sausage and Fennel Parm Heroes, 202
Shrimp and Chorizo Tortas, 204
Smoky Fishwiches, 108
Tuna Banh Mi, 64

SAUSAGE
Boiled Potatoes with Sage Butter, 181
Lentil and Chicken Cassoulet, 150
Orecchiette with Sausage, Chickpeas and Mint, 169
Pork and Sausage Meat Loaf with Cherries, 78
Sausage and Apple Frittata with Dill, 105
Sausage and Cheddar Muffins, 200
Sausage and Fennel Parm Heroes, 202
Sausage Choucroute, 201
Shrimp and Chorizo Tortas, 204
Spaghetti with Brussels Sprout and Sausage Breadcrumbs, 53
Warm Escarole Salad with Sausage Vinaigrette, 203

SCALLIONS
Bulgogi-Style Pepper Steak Sandwiches, 172
Green Bean and Scallion Pancake, 119

SCALLOPS
Scallops with Thai Chile Sauce, 134

SESAME SEEDS
Creamy Sesame-Garlic Tofu Dressing, 227
Snap Pea and Radish Salad with Tahini Dressing, 211

SHRIMP
Angry Shrimp Spaghettini, 206
Baked Shrimp Risotto, 191
Corn-Shrimp Dumplings, 88
Cucumber Gazpacho with Shrimp, 92
Fettuccine with Shrimp, 166
Grilled Shrimp with Shrimp Butter, 207
Shrimp and Chorizo Tortas, 204

Shrimp Cakes with Spicy
Mayo, 206

Shrimp Salad with Green Curry
Dressing, 204

SOUPS

Chicken-Chile Soup, 82

Chipotle–Butternut Squash Soup
with Chive Cream, 54

Creamy Roasted Broccoli Soup, 46

Cucumber Gazpacho with
Shrimp, 92

Fish Soup with Cabbage and
Potatoes, 111

Silky Cauliflower Soup with
Charmoula and Smoked
Almonds, 73

Summery Fresh Tomato Soup, 230

Turkey Curry Soup, 237

Tuscan White Bean and Escarole
Soup with Tuna, 65

SPINACH

Asian Pork Noodles with
Spinach, 214

Indian Fried Rice with Chickpeas
and Spinach, 192

Quinoa with Spinach and Roasted
Almonds, 214

Spinach and Caramelized Onion
Dip, 213

Spinach Salad with Walnut
Vinaigrette, 214

Spinach Spoon Bread, 215

SQUASH. *See also* **BUTTERNUT
SQUASH; ZUCCHINI**

Turkey Curry Soup, 237

STEWS

Chickpea and Swiss Chard Chili, 85

Ham, Escarole and White Bean
Stew, 131

Spring Beef Stew, 35

Turkey and Pinto Bean Chili, 239

STRAWBERRIES

Balsamic Strawberries with
Strawberry Sorbet, 219

Banana-Strawberry Tartines, 30

Caramelized Panzanella with
Strawberries, 216

Fresh Strawberry Sauce, 219

Strawberry-Prosecco Gelées, 217

Strawberry Shortcake, 218

SWEET POTATOES

Baked Sweet Potato Chips, 223

Coconut Lamb Curry with Sweet
Potatoes, 144

Mushroom Poutine, 157

Sweet Potato and Mushroom
Salad, 222

Sweet Potatoes with Almond
Pesto, 222

Sweet Potato Hash Browns, 220

Sweet Potato–Tomato Pasta
Sauce, 220

T

TOFU

Creamy Sesame-Garlic Tofu
Dressing, 227

Crispy Tofu Steaks with Ginger
Vinaigrette, 228

Seared Tofu Tabbouleh, 227

Tofu Masala, 229

Yellow Lentil Dal with Tofu, 148

TOMATOES

Apricot and Ricotta Tartines, 17

Baked Rigatoni with Eggplant,
Tomatoes and Ricotta, 101

Chicken and Pepper Cacciatore, 173

Coconut Curried Beef Noodles, 124

Garlicky Cherry Tomato and Bread
Gratin, 234

Garlic-Toasted Tomato
Tartines, 234

Mexican Eggs Baked in Tomato
Sauce, 102

Mixed Bell Pepper Pasta, 171

Pappardelle with Tomatoes,
Almonds and Parmesan, 232

Quinoa-Pork Meatballs, 187

Roasted Tomatoes with Anchovies
and Capers, 230

Salmon and Cherry Tomato
Skewers with Rosemary
Vinaigrette, 198

Sausage and Fennel Parm
Heroes, 202

Simplest Lamb Bolognese with
Pappardelle, 145

Summery Fresh Tomato Soup, 230

Sweet Potato–Tomato Pasta
Sauce, 220

Tofu Masala, 229

Tomato Salad with Horseradish
Ranch Dressing, 233

Turkey and Pinto Bean Chili, 239

Yellow Lentil Dal with Tofu, 148

TUNA

Herb-Marinated Peppers and
Tuna, 171

Lemony Tuna and Artichoke
Dip, 66

Tuna Banh Mi, 64

Tuna Escabeche Tostadas, 66

Turkey Tonnato, 237

Tuscan White Bean and Escarole
Soup with Tuna, 65

TURKEY

Turkey and Pinto Bean Chili, 239

Turkey Curry Soup, 237

Turkey Reuben Hash, 238

Turkey-Stuffing Salad, 238

Turkey Tonnato, 237

Y

YOGURT

Egg Salad with Herbs and
Pickles, 103

Grilled Halibut Dip, 110

Spinach and Caramelized Onion
Dip, 213

Turkey Tonnato, 237

Z

ZUCCHINI

Carrot, Coconut and Zucchini
Bread, 70

Crispy Zucchini Pancakes, 245

Grilled Zucchini and Lamb with
Serrano Chile, 245

Zucchini Confetti Pasta with Dill
and Walnuts, 242

Zucchini Gratin, 242

More Books from Food & Wine

Annual Cookbook More than 650 recipes from the world's best cooks, including culinary legends Jacques Pépin and Alice Waters as well as star chefs like Bobby Flay, Alex Guarnaschelli and Giada De Laurentiis.

Best of the Best More than 100 delicious recipes from the 25 best cookbooks of the year, chosen by FOOD & WINE after rigorous testing. Plus, more than 20 exclusive, never-before-published recipes.

Cocktails Over 150 new and classic recipes from America's most brilliant bartenders. Plus, an indispensable guide to cocktail basics and the top new bars and lounges around the country.

To order, call 800-284-4145 or visit foodandwine.com/books